Heaven, Hell
and
Near-Death Experiences

Proof of Life After Death

By Eric A. Folds

ISBN: 978-1-62999-118-4

Printed in the United States of America

Scripture quotations are from the King James Version of the Bible as well as the 1981 Version of The Living Bible. All rights reserved. The information should enable the reader to compare experiences studied by research teams to the biblical description of Heaven and Hell.

Author's Note: This book is written to spread information on the truth in regards to life after death and to provide insight into the phenomena of such experiences. The book is for scholarship, educational, nonprofit, and informational purposes. The author is not engaged in rendering any professional services to the reader. If the reader requires personal assistance and advice, a competent professional should be consulted. The author's intent is to spread the Gospel of Jesus Christ to every possible city, town, village, and country, and to support tax exempt, religious or charitable organizations. The content of the book is the sole opinion of the author based on The Word of God, the leading of the Holy Spirit, and the words of Jesus Christ Himself. All of the information contained in the book have been shared in the ministry and have been maintained in notes from sermons prepared for research and educational purposes for parishioners of tax exempt, nonprofit charitable organizations. All proceeds are designated for donation to a nonprofit organization. This book could be used as an aid in evangelism.

TABLE OF CONTENTS

Chapter One

Heaven, Hell and Near-Death Experiences, Proof of Life after Death

The proof of life after death, Heaven and Hell are enormous. Near-death studies is a field of psychology and psychiatry that studies the near-death experience and the phenomenology and the after effects. It is estimated that over 2% of the population has had a near-death experience. Many people have similar experiences after the final heartbeat once they are out of the body before they return to the body. They have a review of their life. There is an encounter with a spiritual being such as an angel or demon that occurs. There is sometimes a decision by oneself or someone else such as an angelic being for them to return to their physical body. There is the experience of the individual to see their dead body in the hospital and from above the body (while floating in air above the body) and it is normally later shared with those who were alive during that time. Patients that returned from death stated to researchers of near-death experiences that they were in Hell (Dr. Rommer, 2000, p.42). Others have stated that they were in Heaven. They also stated after returning from death that the heat was really something (Greyson and Bush, 1992, p.100). Scientific research teams have proven the reality of Heaven and Hell. Many people who had these experiences felt it was a warning (Bush,2002).

Bruce Greyson is the Director of the Division of Perceptual Studies, Department of Psychiatry at the University of Virginia. The Department has studied the science of postmortem survival and case after case of people who survived death for decades. The mind (soul) survives after death of the physical body. Bruce Greyson and Nancy Evans Bush (1992) in Distressing Near-Death Experiences, Psychiatry, Volume 55, Page 109 mentioned that the third type of near-death experience is the "hellish" type. The hellish type from the research compiled occurs when the heart stops beating and a clinically death occurs. The soul floats out of the body. They hear sounds of torment and images that are hellish and have encounters with demonic beings. Sometimes a guide such as an angel may accompany the individual through the experience. We should keep in mind that to prove or disprove anything, you need witnesses. The witnesses prove it. Rawlings (1978), Garfield (1979), Moody (1979) and Grey (1985) found from interviews of those who returned from death that the experiences of the patients were consistent with what our Bibles call Hell or Heaven depending upon who is being interviewed. The experience of patients that regained a heartbeat varied. Interestingly enough, Irwin and Bramwell (1988) reported in their findings that a near-death experience started out as positive, such as the dead patient remembering that they were floating out of the body and to a light, but then the experience turned negative and involved frightening encounters with demonic beings. When you really think about it, "Satan masquerades as if he were an angel of the light" (2 Corinthians 11:14). The Apostle Paul in our Bibles mentions that he had an experience of traveling to the third heaven and saw things which were forbidden to be uttered.

He mentioned that he did not know whether he was in the body or out of it (2 Corinthians 12:2-5). The blackness and eternal void was seen and experienced by some who traveled out of body after death before returning. The blackness and eternal void experienced in the research data seems to parallel to Jesus' own words in regards to the afterlife and in my opinion that of one being thrown into outer darkness (Matthew 25:30). Some survivors described traveling through a tunnel or toward an abyss or pit. Others described moving toward a light and feeling unconditionally loved. John described in his vision, "And I saw an angel come down from heaven, having the key to the bottomless pit, and a great chain in his hand. And he laid hold on the dragon, that old serpent, which is the Devil, and Satan, and bound him a thousand years. And cast him into the bottomless pit, and shut him up, and set a seal upon him, that he should deceive the nations no more, till the thousand years should be fulfilled (Revelation 20:1- 3). Satan will be locked up into the bottomless pit for one thousand years after the end of this age and prior to going to the Lake of Fire described later in Revelation. We later read, "And the devil that deceived them was cast into the Lake of fire and brimstone, where the beast and the false prophet are, and shall be tormented day and night forever and ever" (Revelation 20:10). At this time the Devil is on the earth prowling around like a lion and seeking who he can destroy (I Peter 5:8). Jesus came to deliver us from Satan's strong grip on our souls.

Bruce Greyson (psychiatrist), Kenneth Ring (psychologist), Michael Sabom (cardiologist) and Melvin Morse (pediatrician) introduced the study of Near-Death experiences to the academic world. The International Association of Near-Death Studies was founded in 1981. Ring published his book in 1980 called *Life at Death: A Scientific Investigation of the Near-Death Experience*. The organization which preceded (IANDS) was called the Association for the Scientific Study of Near Death Phenomena. The researchers who formulated that group were John Audette, Raymond Moody, Bruce Greyson, Kenneth Ring, and Michael Sabom. The British Researcher and Neuro-Psychiatrist Peter Tenwich started to collect stories from people who died and later returned to their bodies in the 1980's. The psychiatrist presented his findings on television back in 1981. Over 3,400 cases have been reviewed and studied by psychiatrists and psychologists between 1975 and 2005. There have been over 50 research teams. The first conference of the International Association of Near-Death Studies was at Yale University, New Haven, CT in 1982. A book was published in 2009 by Praeger Publications called *The Handbook of Near-Death Experiences: Thirty Years of Investigation,* a comprehensive critical review of the research carried out within the field of near-death studies. The world has many witnesses and scientific proof that life continues after death. It is safe to conclude without speculation that heaven and hell are real. We should believe this because Jesus revealed it in his Word.

When you review all of the data studied by scholars to include psychiatrists, psychologists, and many others for more than three decades, you can also easily conclude that there is life after death and that there is a heaven and a hell as described by the Bible. The science of postmortem survival has confirmed what the Bible has been teaching for centuries. We have a soul that survives death of the physical body. A lot has been discovered and there is still a lot to be explored and much unknown. Most who returned from death know for sure that physical death is not the end of life. Some recollect events that happened after physical death that they could not have known unless they were alive and outside of the body and had actually arrived in heaven. In some cases people died and returned after being brought back to life, and they reported that they saw a relative in heaven that nobody knew at that time was dead. After the near-death experiences of this type, the family later discovered that this relative had indeed recently passed away. What could possibly be the explanation for such phenomena, except that the soul survives death of the physical body?

Bruce Greyson developed the Near-Death experience scale. The item scale was found to have high consistency, test reliability, retest reliability, and split-half reliability. Thousands have had valid experiences which prove life after death. Greyson and Bush (1996) put the out of the body with near-death experience into three types. The most commonly reported experience after the heart stopped beating is the out of the body experience of rapid movement of going downward as through a tunnel or toward a light. There is the feeling of being out of control while traveling through the tunnel combined with raw terror.

The second is the awareness of being alone or having a void. I want you to know that with this type many patients that died in the hospital felt that they had been tricked. Some could hear demonic entities insult them and things were said out of malice and from a very evil entity. They felt they were victims of malice and torment by an evil spirit.

The third type was called "hellish" and fits the description of Hell. There is a very ugly landscape and the presence of demonic beings which can be seen. There are frightening creatures and people are in extreme regret and terror moaning in pain or screaming (Rawlings, 1978).

The fourth type of near-death experience is an out of body experience after death. There is reported a feeling of a Higher Power, such as God judging the person having the near-death experience (Rommer 2000). The person experiencing the fourth type feels unconditionally loved, but no reported encounters with demonic beings. Many reported that they were in heaven and that they did not want to return. Our Bibles teach us that God is love (I John 4:8). Jesus loves us and died for our sins (John 3:16).

(Zaleski Carol.1987) provided us with "Otherworld Journeys: Accounts Near-Death experiences in Medieval and Modern Times" from the Oxford University Press. Many New Agers found her work to be disturbing because they thought the out of body experience did not include accountability for this life and judgment from God. They found the opposite to be the truth from her research. The out of body experiences that can occur when one is alive is significantly different from what is experienced upon death. There is a striking parallel between experiences centuries before and modern day out of the body experiences upon death. (Greyson B., and Stevenson, I. 1980 137:1193-1196) gave us "The phenomenology of near- death experiences" in the American Journal of psychiatry.

Bush (2002) observed that people who had a near death experience and returned to their bodies felt that it was a warning. They were able to see the consequences of previous behaviors they identified as being bad, and they also found ways to change their lives (p. 104). Bonefant, R.J (2001) wrote to us about a child's encounter with the devil and said it was an unusual near-death experience for a child with blissful and frightening elements. See the Journal of Near Death Studies 20(2), p. 87-100. There is proof of life after death as described by witnesses for many decades throughout the world that left their bodies and had encounters with demonic beings and a hellish experience. Hell has also been proven by a qualitative and quantitative study of the out of body experience, features, and aetiology of near death experiences in cardiac arrest survivors (Parnia, S., Waller, D.G. Yeates R., E Fenwick P. 2001). See Resuscitation 48, p. 149-156. The event such as floating out of the body and giving accurate details of one's own cardiac arrest and events after death are things which a person who is clinically dead cannot see, and they are definitely impossible to give an explanation for except that there is a conscious soul outside of the body (Morse and Perry, 1990, p.169).

Research proves that some, but not all survivors of heart attacks had what we call an out of body experience and encounters with demonic beings, which were not friendly (Greyson and Bush 1996) and (Schwaninger, J., Eisenberg, P.R, Schechtman, KB. E Weiss A.N. 2002). We can conclude that Heaven and Hell are real places based on Jesus' own words if you are a Christian believer. If you are not, once you read the books of the experts that documented what they learned from scientific studies and interviews of the survival souls after death, you will have no other choice but to conclude that heaven and hell are real. See "a prospective analysis of near-death experiences in cardiac arrest patients." Check the Journal of Near Death Studies 20(4), p. 215- 232. Hell is a very real place and in some instances people can recall seeing everything that happened in the emergency room after leaving the body and after they were pronounced dead. They sometimes recall being surrounded by demons and seeing others in a place of torment.

Some survivors have a post-traumatic effect and go into intense psychotherapy after they return to the body. The people who have an extraordinary experience have a deepened sense of spiritual meaning associated with the out of body experience, even if they were previously atheists. Some atheists convert to Christianity. The International Association of Near Death Studies have developed support groups for anyone who has had a Near Death experience in order for them to get psychological support from a group of peers who have experienced the same encounters. Ladies and Gentlemen, I am reporting to you that Heaven and Hell are real and that Jesus Christ died for your sins. He rose again on the third day to save you from punishment in

Hell. Believe him for your salvation and repent of sins. Confess that Jesus is Lord and ask him to save you from your sins. He can forgive you if you repent and believe. At the time of the writing of this book about 155,000 people are dying every day. Everybody won't make it back and everybody doesn't go to Heaven. Jesus is the only way, and he loves us unconditionally.

The person who had a distressing near-death experience or what is called the Hell experience said they had a major change in values, attitudes and beliefs (Greyson and Stevenson 1980; Noyes 1980; Ring 1980, 1984; Sabom 1982; Grey 1985; Flynn 1986; Raft and Andresen 1986; Atwater 1988; Roberts and Owen 1988). Lindley, Bryan, and Conky (1981) in a study of the near-death and out of body experiences found many of them to be hellish. They defined a negative one as mental anguish, desperation, intense loneliness, and desolation. She found the environment of the experiencer to be dark and hostile; often subjects reported as being on the brink of a pit or abyss. She further defined the hell experiencers to have experienced the presence of an evil force such as threatening demonic creatures. Grey reported that the distressful near death experience of life after death has the sequence of 1) Fear and panic 2) The out of the body experience in which the patient at the hospital can look down and see their body dead. 3) Entering a black void or tunnel. 4) Seeing and sensing demons 5) Entering Hell or what they called a hellish experience. Atwater (1988) described some experiences of those who died as having a sense of the reality of being in Hell and the other as having encounters with friendly beings, a beautiful environment, conversations, acceptance and love, warmth, and a feeling of being in heaven. Patients who had an out of the body experience after being clinically dead reported sounds of torments and encounters with demonic beings. The experiences of these patients in Hell varied based on research done by Raw-

lings (1978), Garfield (1979), and Grey (1985). Irwin and Bramwell (1988) reported a near death experience that began to un-
fold as a positive one but then evolved into a frightening one with
demonic beings. It was as if the demonic entity had fooled them
into thinking that they were on their way to heaven and then to
drag them toward Hell.

The people who have experienced a near-death experience of
the fourth type as described by Rommer (2000) had a review of
their life after death with an encounter with a Higher Power and
being unconditionally loved. This, in my opinion, has similarities
to the biblical account of what happens in eternity. They reported
that they felt unconditionally loved near God, which is consistent with the Bible's definition of God. God is love (I John 4:20).
The Apostle John wrote, "I saw a Great White Throne and the
one enthroned. Nothing could stand before or against the Presence, nothing in Heaven, nothing on earth. And then I saw all
the dead, great and small, standing there--before the Throne!
And books were opened. Then another book was opened: the
Book of Life. The dead were judged by what was written in the
books by the way they had lived. Sea released its dead, Death and
Hell turned in their dead. Each man and woman was judged by
the way he or she lived. Then death and Hell were hurled into the
Lake of Fire. This is the second death-Lake Fire. Anyone whose
name was not found inscribed in the Book of Life was hurled
into the Lake of Fire (Revelation 20:11-15). The scholars have
made scientific studies of both the good and bad experiences of
life after death reported by those who died and returned to life
again. The similarities with the biblical revelation are similar, in
my opinion, because of the feeling of being judged and having a
review of their own life. However, the Great White Throne judgment occurs in eternity in a time that is yet future tense and after
death. The scriptures teach, "It is appointed to men once to die

and after that the judgment" (Hebrews 9:27). Theologians have for centuries held the position that after death the soul enters into eternity. Jesus spoke a parable of a Rich Man that entered into Hell into torment in a flame and a beggar that entered into a peaceful place of comfort (Luke 16:19-31). Rommer (2000) identified that those who had near-death experiences had a life review and a feeling of being judged by a Higher Power. They also felt unconditionally loved at a depth not possible on earth. Scholarly research has been done for decades on the distressing near-death experiences.

What is heaven really like? The most credible and descriptive documented vision of heaven ever is that by John. "The city shined like a precious gem, light-filled, pulsing light. The wall was majestic and high with twelve gates. At each gate stood an Angel, and on the gates were inscribed the names of the Twelve Tribes of the sons of Israel: three gates to the east, three gates on the north, three on the south, three on the west. The wall was set on twelve foundations, the names of the Twelve Apostles of the Lamb inscribed on them. The angel speaking with me had a gold measuring stick to measure the City, its gates, and its wall. The City was laid out in a perfect square. He measured the City with a measuring stick: twelve thousand stadia, its length, width, and height all equal. Using the standard measure, The Angel measured the thickness of its wall: 144 cubits. The wall was jasper, the color of Glory, and the City was pure Gold, translucent as glass. The foundations of the City walls were garnished with every precious gem imaginable: the first foundation jasper: the second sapphire, the third agate, the fourth emerald, the fifth onyx, the sixth carnelian, the seventh chrysolite, the eighth beryl, the ninth topaz, the tenth chrysoprase, the eleventh jacinth, the twelfth amethyst. The twelve gates were twelve pearls, each gate a single pearl. The main street of the City was pure gold. But there was no sign of a Temple, for the Lord God and the Lamb are the temple. The City does not need a sun or a moon for light, the Lamb is the Light. The nations will walk in its light and the earth's kings bring in their splendor. Its gates will never be shut by day and there won't be any night. They will bring the glory and honor of the nations into the City. Nothing that is dirty or defiled will get into the City, and no one does abominations or works lies. Only those whose names are written in the Lamb's Book of Life will get in. Then the angel showed me the pure river of the water of life, crystal bright. The river flowed from the Throne of God and the Lamb right down the middle of the street. The Tree of Life was planted on each side of the river, producing twelve kinds of fruit, a ripe fruit each month. The leaves of the tree are for healing the nations. Nothing will ever be cursed again. The Throne of God and the Lamb are at the center. The servants of God will worship, looking on his face, their foreheads honoring him. Never again will there be sunlight. The shining of God, the Master, is all the light anyone needs. They will rule the earth for the ages" (Revelation 21:9-22:5). John's description of Heaven warns us that certain types of people will not enter into Heaven which is consistent with what has been discovered by the near-death experience research teams. Some have the Heaven experience and others have the "hellish" experience prior to regaining a heartbeat, which parallels to what is revealed in John's vision in the Bible. The science of postmortem survival proved a Heaven and Hell type of experience after death. There is surely a warning in John's vision that the people who continued to practice abominations and lies could not enter into this beautiful city. The earth is apparently a place of testing, temptation, and trials. The next life is a place of rewards and consequences. Supernatural or what we can call other-worldly help will be needed to get to Heaven. The angelic guide will know us. The angels shall separate the wheat from the tares (Matthew 13:37-43).

A Finland Newspaper wrote an article that revealed a team of geologists and researchers recorded the screams and cries of the damned. Dr. Azzacove, the lead geologist said, "As a communist I don't believe in heaven or the Bible, but as a scientist, I now believe in hell. We are absolutely certain that we have drilled through the very gates of hell. The drill suddenly began to rotate wildly, indicating that we had reached a large empty pocket or cavern. Temperature sensors showed a dramatic increase in heat to 2,000 degrees Fahrenheit. We lowered a microphone designed to detect the sounds of plate movements down the shaft, but instead of plate movements, we heard a human voice screaming in pain! At first we thought it was our own equipment, but when we made adjustments, our worst suspicions were confirmed. The screams weren't those of a single human, they were the screams and cries and millions." God loves us. It is because he loves that he warns us about the dangers of hellfire and eternal damnation. Jesus warned, "Fear not them which kill the body, but are not able to kill the soul: but rather fear him which is able to destroy both soul and body in hell" (Matthew 10:28).

Bruce Greyson and Nancy Evans Bush, President of the International Association of Near Death Studies completed a descriptive study of terrifying cases of Near Death Studies that they collected over a period of nine years (Greyson and Bush 1992). Bruce Greyson has been the professor of psychiatry and Director of the Division of perceptual studies. He has been the long term editor of the Journal of Near Death Studies and the largest contributor to near death research. He wrote the near death experiences chapter in Varieties of Anomolies Experiences (2000). Others who work has proved the reality of a Hell experienced after death include the British researcher Margot Grey (1985) and sociologist Charles Flynn (1986) and the list of Medical Doctors,

Psychiatrists, and other professionals goes on. The professors of psychiatry and scientific research teams may not have called it Hell, but what they described that patients saw and experienced after death fits the Biblical description of Hell, especially descriptions of the patients' experience described by Dr. Rawlings (1978). People in the near death studies died and prior to regaining a heartbeat they experienced threatening encounters with apparitions after death. They heard screams and cries of people tormented. Many felt abandoned and many felt high temperature increases and felt like they were being punished. Numerous people reported being chased by a devil that physically manifested himself to the dead person. The manifestation of other creatures was reported to be similar to those depicted in the movie *Flatliners* (Schumacher, 1993). Hell is real and researchers around the world have proven that because of all of the witnesses that have died and went to Hell prior to regaining a heartbeat. There is no other explanation as to how someone can leave the body and observe everything happening in the emergency room from elsewhere when they are clinically dead. There is life after death. Pick one. Heaven or Hell.

Dr. Maurice Rawlings was a specialist in internal medicine, and he published a book by the title of *Beyond Death's Door*. He was formerly an atheist until 1977 when he was resuscitating a man who was terrified and screaming that he was going down into the flames of Hell. Dr. Rawlings stated in his book, "Each time he regained a heartbeat and respiration, the patient screamed, "I am in hell." He was terrified and pleaded with me to help him. I was scared to death. Then I noticed a genuinely alarmed look on his face. He had a look worse than the expression seen in death. The pupils were dilated, and he was perspiring and trembling. He looked as if his hair was "on end."

Dr. Rawlings is now a devoted Christian. The book he published describes the reality of Hell that many saw after death on the operating table before they regained a heartbeat. *Beyond Death's Door*, Rawlings' first book (1978) focused on his observations of people being resuscitated after clinical death. Dr. Rawlings explained the numerous stories that people had of being surrounded by unpleasant grotesque human and animal forms, violent and demonic types of torture, and the fact that they heard other people moaning in pain. Most of these people did not believe in God, Bible, or hell prior to the near death experience. Jesus taught his disciples by saying, "And if thy eye offend thee, pluck it out: it is better to enter into the kingdom of God with one eye, than having two eyes to be cast into the fire" (Mark 9:47). It means you must let some excess baggage go and change.

The warning from Jesus implies that the disciples must deny themselves and the lustful passions which war against the soul. The same verse is quoted by Jesus in the ninth chapter of the book of Matthew after his statement on adultery. Jesus said, "You have heard that is was said by them of old time, thou shall not commit adultery: But I say unto you, that whosoever looketh on a woman to lust after her hath committed adultery with her already in his heart" (Matthew 5:27-28). Jesus then says that it is better to enter into heaven with one eye than to have your whole body cast into hell (Matthew 5:29). It is clear in these passages of scripture that what we do on the earth with our bodies and our conduct will play a role in where we spend eternity after death. Admit that you have been wrong, repent by changing your mind and turning from sin, and ask Jesus to forgive you and to save you from sin and God's wrath in Hell.

Scientists have determined that the center of the earth is a burning hot fire that is hotter than the sun. In the Birmingham News, April 10, 1987, they had an article entitled, The Earth's Center is Hotter than the Sun's Surface, Scientists say." The article stated that the scientists had recently discovered that the inner core of the earth has a temperature of over 12,000 degrees Fahrenheit. Thousands of years ago, the Bible described a place located underneath the earth that was a prison for lost souls and the damned that were burning in a lake of fire and brimstone day and night. Jesus described Hell as a place where the fire would not be quenched and where the worm would not die. Jesus described that he would go into the heart of the earth after he died (Matthew 12:40). Paul described to the church of Ephesus that Jesus went underneath the earth (Ephesians 4:9). Peter described on the day of Pentecost that the soul of Jesus would not stay in Hell (Acts 2:29-31). Long before scientists made these discoveries in regards to the core of the earth being a burning hot river inside of the center of the earth it was revealed in the Bible.

Casper Peucer, a fourteenth century astronomer and physician, and Harold Sigurdson, the author of Melting the Earth; The History of Ideas on Volcanic Eruptions, and many others have documented many cases of screams and cries coming out of volcanoes which echoed and they concluded that it had to be the screams and cries of the damned in hell below. Scientists also discovered cracks on the earth's ocean floor where fire was leaking out with giant tube worm crawling near the fire. Jesus described Hell as being a place where the worm did not die and the fire was not quenched (Mark 9:48). I have heard people preach on Hell before, and they sometimes give the title of the sermon in the form of a question and ask "What in Hell do you want?" I don't know that anyone would actually want anything in Hell, but I have been persuaded that many people really don't believe that Hell is real.

Many people have had near death experiences and have returned after regaining a heartbeat. They have recalled events of being surrounded by grotesque human and animal forms, hearing other people moaning in pain and being tormented in a hell-like experience. Some of the researchers who have studied such experiences include the British researcher Margot Grey (1985) and sociologist Charles Flynn (1986). The proof that Hell is real is enormous. As you consider the fact that geologist say they dug into Hell consider that the Bible says, "They dig into Hell" (Amos 9:2). Amos was a prophet during biblical days who foretold events to come in the future.

A Pastor in Africa was raised from the dead after being dead for days. He was raised from the dead after the church prayed for him in a Sunday school room at a revival held by the German Evangelist Reinhart Bonnke. Everyone knows that the story of the resurrection is true because of the many eyewitnesses to the event. He also was pronounced dead and had a death certificate and was embalmed. After the fatal car accident he was pronounced dead by an African Doctor, and he had no pulse or heartbeat and a death certificate was issued. The Pastor's wife kept believing that God would raise him and days later had his body transported to the revival held by the German Evangelist. After the church prayed and after he was raised from the dead as a result of prayer in Jesus' name he told everyone his story of the angel showing him both heaven and hell while he was dead. He also mentioned that if he had not returned to the earth that he would have been sent to Hell for eternity for not forgiving his wife. Hell is a real place. I encourage everyone to read the story of Pastor Daniel Ekechukwu on your own or to find his entire story and hear the eyewitnesses online regarding the horrors of hell he saw. He was dead for days prior to being resurrected in Africa. Please also consider what Jesus said about forgiveness. Jesus said, "But if you forgive not men of their trespasses, neither will your heavenly Father forgive your trespasses" (Matthew 6:15).

A Christian cardiologist named Dr. Chauncey Crandall produced proof of the resurrection of one of his own patients from the dead at the fourth Annual World Christian Doctor's Network conference in Miami, Florida. The patient was raised due to the prayer of faith by Dr. Crandall. The patient described some of the horrors he experienced after his final heartbeat prior to being brought back to life by the Christian Cardiologist. Hell is a place where we remain conscious of our existence, and we remember our lives upon the earth. Jesus asks of us to repent and to believe him. Jesus said, "God so loved the world that he gave his only begotten son that whosoever believes in him should not perish but have eternal life" (John 3:16). Repenting of sin is a change of one's mind resulting in a change of conduct and belief because of a godly and heartfelt sorrow for our thoughts, deeds, and ways because they break God's laws and his commandments. We can be saved from the flames of hell if we repent and believe the gospel in our hearts. We must confess with our mouth that Jesus is Lord and believe within our hearts that he died for our sins on the cross and rose from the dead on the third day (Romans 10:9).

Archaeologists and explorers have also discovered the ruined cities of Sodom and Gomorrah. Many other researchers, archaeologists and explorers have been through the city. The Bible describes those cities as surrounding the Dead Sea. Archaeologists have identified those cities. The limestone buildings were destroyed by brimstone, which fell from the sky. The terms, "sulfur and brimstone" are one and the same. The Bible says, "The Lord rained upon Sodom and upon Gomorrah fire and brimstone out of heaven" (Gen. 19:24). Researchers found no evidence of volcanic activity around these ancient cities, and brimstone is normally mined out of Geo-thermal locations. The cities are still covered today in piles of ash with pure balls of brimstone within the ruins, which have been turned into ashes. Skeletal remains were discovered which were destroyed by fire. There are no other cities anywhere in the world that have been turned into ashes as was Sodom and Gomorrah. It is true that the Roman city of Pompeii had a layer of ash on top of the limestone buildings which came from a volcanic eruption; however, there are no other ancient cities in the world today like Sodom and Gomorrah, which have been turned into ash by brimstone balls that fell from the sky. The brimstone that comes from volcanoes is only about 40% brimstone in comparison to the brimstone from Sodom, which is 98% brimstone. There is no other place on the earth where 98% brimstone still remains as in the piles of ashes throughout Sodom. The ash in Sodom and Gomorrah today where the brimstone remains proves that the Bible is true. He turned the cities of Sodom and Gomorrah to ashes to leave them as an example and reminder to those that would live in the same or similar ungodly way, as to what was going to happen to them (2 Pet. 2:6).

It is not possible to build an entire city completely out of ash. Wood that burns cannot turn a limestone building to ash by itself. They tested the white ashes throughout the cities of Sodom and Gomorrah and found that this ash was calcium sulfate. You can only get calcium sulfate with brimstone and limestone from the ancient limestone buildings burning together with brimstone. This proves that both cities were destroyed by the brimstone raining down from the sky to burn the cities, just as the Bible says. The fires started on rooftops in the cities.

The limestone buildings, which were turned into ashes, are still standing in place in the original design except that they are completely ash. A sphinx-shaped pyramid is also completely ash and stands in the original design. Researchers have proven that they could have only turned to ash by thermal ionization. Thermal ionization occurs when something burns at several thousands degrees Fahrenheit. The brimstone that was tested that hit these ancient buildings and was extracted from the ashes would have had to be over 4000 degrees Fahrenheit in order to turn them into ashes, according to researchers. As they dug through the ashes throughout Sodom and Gomorrah, they found brimstone balls buried in the ashes throughout the city and within the structures that were turned into ash. There is no place else on the planet where you can find any brimstone in such a pure form, nor any physical structure which looks like it was built from the ground up made entirely out of ash. Explorers have also discovered human bodies, which had been literally fried inside of the remains of these cities. These ruins of Sodom, which have been discovered, prove that God did rain fire out of the sky to destroy them because of the wickedness that was in them. If you or I could travel to these cities by the Dead Sea today, we would be able to see with our own eyes and walk through the piles of ashes throughout the city near what appears to be buildings that were turned into ash. We could run our fingers through some brimstone and peel off some of the ash from the buildings including elongated pyramid structures near the temple site in Gomorrah.

The ash in Sodom and Gomorrah was subjected to intense heat by researchers, but the heat couldn't change the colors of the ashes because it had already been consumed. The substances burned with brimstone have a heavier ash weight than the original substance. This explains why what appears to be buildings composed completely of ash on the inside and out have remained standing for centuries. The layers of ash were twisted and warped by intense heat and settled into a form that resembles the original object. The lack of rainfall in the area contributes to the longevity of the ash buildings that remain in the same shape as the original structures, which were limestone. Over in Gomorrah there are two elongated pyramids that highlight the entry into the temple site of Gomorrah that are still standing at a 90-degree angle and are entirely ash. These are literal monuments in ashes.

The Bible says that Lot's wife looked back and was turned into a pillar of salt. There is a pillar near the ruins of Sodom and Gomorrah that resembles the human body of a woman that is currently identified and referred to as Lot's wife. We can't say for certain that this pillar of salt really is her, but it has been identified as and referred to as Lot's wife because it resembles to some degree a human body turned into a pillar of salt. Because the Bible tells us that these cities were destroyed by God raining fire and brimstone from the sky and were turned to ashes, and the fact that archaeologists have found the ruins of these cities with the brimstone, thousands of tons of ashes throughout the cities, buildings, pyramids, and structures turned into ash. This alone is proof enough of the accuracy of the biblical record. It proves that God is a God of judgment and fire, and that He has a Lake of Fire that burns with brimstone, which He has as a final judgment for each sinner that won't repent. The Bible says, "But the fearful, and the unbelieving, and the abominable, and murderers, and whoremongers, and sorcerers, and idolaters, and all liars, shall have their part in the lake which burns with fire and brimstone: which is the second death" (Rev. 21:8). Let us consider the truth about the discoveries of Sodom and Gomorrah. The Bible says, "And turning the cities of Sodom and Gomorrah into ashes condemned them with an overthrow, making them an example unto those that after should live ungodly" (II Peter 2:6). The churches, nations, and sinners must repent of all ungodliness. The ancient cities which have been discovered were left by God for us as examples of how the judgment of God will be poured out on each unrepentant sinner by fire and brimstone. Jesus is the only way for us to get saved from the wrath of God in Hell. Jesus said, "For God so loved the world, that he gave his only begotten Son, that whosoever believeth in him should not perish, but hath everlasting life. The scriptures teach, "For God sent not his son into the world to condemn the world; but that the world through him might be saved" (John 3:16-17). Jesus came in order that the world can be saved. He said, "He that believes on him is not condemned: but he that believeth not is condemned already, because he hath not believed in the name of the only begotten Son of God" (John 3:18).

Chapter Two

Proof of Satan

Exorcisms, OBE's, Therapy & Deliverance

How can anyone prove that Satan is real? If you find that Satan is prowling around and trying to harm you what will you do? We know that exorcisms have taken place for centuries and not just in America but everywhere. The Catholic Church has had several exorcists (people who cast out the devil) in the United States. They report the same type of bizarre behavior in records that we see on the movies to include levitations, supernatural strength displayed by the person who needs deliverance, the speaking of demons through the person, mysterious wounds, the utterance of words that are hateful against people or God. The Roman Catholic exorcisms are elaborate and carefully planned rituals. Hundreds of other exorcisms are performed by people of faith in various religious organizations or groups. We also know that many claim to be a worshipper of the devil. Moreover, many who had near-death experiences also had an out of the body experience which included an encounter with a demonic being and recall being in a place called Hell (Rawlings, 1978).

Dr. Edith Fiore (1987) published a book on spirit attachment.

Her book, *The Unquiet Dead*, proved that spirits attached to her clients. The Spirit Attachment was the term used to describe the spiritual entities working through her clients. She found that the spirits affected the thoughts, emotions, and behaviors. Her work was the result of past life regression therapy. The inconsistencies she discovered in past life regression therapy proved that the past lives of her clients were actually the past experiences of disembodied spirits. It is my opinion that they are spirits (demons) which were housed in people who thought they had a previous life on earth. The estimation was that about 70% of all clients have had at least one spirit (demon) attached to them (Guiley, 1991). She believed that the spirits were earthbound spirits of the dead and what we normally refer to as ghosts. The people who had them surely remembered the life of others who had lived on the earth before them in the past. They sometimes believed that they were those people in a previous life. Jesus mentioned that it was a demon that enters a body and looked to take seven more wicked demons with it to live in that body (Matthew 12:43-45).

The British psychiatrist, Arthur Guirdham, M.D., concluded from over 40 years of practice that severe mental illnesses were caused by spirit (demon) interference (Fiore, 1987). Edith Fiore experienced great success with her clients as a result of getting the disembodied spirits out of them. We then got Dr. William Baldwin developing Spirit Releasement Therapy (SRT). Baldwin explained that the spirits were sometimes earthbound spirits inside of the client which we call ghosts. They were said to be the ones who identified with someone on earth and attached to them instead of moving into the next realm. Baldwin also explained that the spirits that were in some clients were sometimes demons who described themselves as such who were fallen angels that followed Lucifer (Satan, the Devil) before he was ousted out of heaven. The demons that identified themselves as such also did under many circumstances where clients had no religious background or association with churches.

The third type of possession that Baldwin encountered in his depossession therapy, which he later called Spirit Releasement Therapy was when the spirits called themselves extraterrestrials. This type of spirit claimed to be inside the person on a mission and from far away. He went on to say that the demonic beings caused a lot of pain, suffering, chaos, destruction, and death. The exorcisms involved identifying the spirit(s) dialogue with the entities, releasing the spirit, sealing-light meditation, and ongoing therapy (Baldwin,1991). Baldwin explained the process of getting the demon out. It was acknowledged that spiritual entities were controlling the clients. One thing for sure is that it is proven that many clients of therapists and professionally trained psychologists and psychiatrists have a demon inside.

Satan masquerades as an angel of light (II Corinthians 11:14). A demon brings many other wicked spirits into the same body (Matthew 12:43-45). Satan is also the Father of lies (John 8:44). It should not surprise us if demons are claiming to be ghosts or posing as aliens from a distant galaxy traveling here to help our civilization.

The healing ministry of Jesus involved casting demons out of those whom Satan had a stronghold on. I am not against therapy, but I know that if the practitioner doesn't have authority to get the demon out that the client can't be cured. Jesus gave his disciples this authority and said, "These signs shall follow them that believe; In my name shall they cast out devils; they shall speak with new tongues" (Mark 16:17). Demons often don't want others to know that they are present in the thoughts, mind, imagination, and subconscious of people. They know if they can avoid detection and escape observation that they can continue to hold the soul into bondage. I routinely pray and command demons to leave the mind, thoughts, and souls of everyone before I minister in churches.

Dr. Carl Wickland, an American physician and psychologist became the first medically trained person to view mental illnesses as being demon possession (Guile, 1991). He wrote extensively in regards to humanity being surrounded by millions of spiritual entities. He also mentioned that the demons were the cause of most of our tantrums, unreasonable impulses, bad moods, negative thoughts processes, and many other problems. Carl Wickland is the author of *Thirty Years Among the Dead*. Jesus mentioned that when the unclean spirit leaves a man that it then returns with seven more demons more wicked than the first and the last state of the man is worse than the first (Matthew 12:43- 45). Getting your demons out is important and keeping them out is important. The prayer for deliverance from Satan in Jesus' name by one of faith can bring an immediate transformation and deliverance in your thoughts, emotions, attitudes, and behaviors if your soul has been manipulated or influenced by Satan. One reason that we must repent and change our mind in regards to sin is to surrender our thoughts, emotions, mind, and body to God. Satan will attempt to use his demons to gain control over areas of our imagination, thoughts, mind, and body once we have been set free. Repentance is your way of deciding that you no longer will be influenced by the demonic beings nor to surrender your thoughts or mind to them but to Jesus instead. Each decision we make can open a door for The Devil or a demon to gain access to our minds or bodies. We have often seen in movies such as Paranormal Activity how that playing with occult objects such as a Ouija board can open a portal for a demon to enter a home.

Please understand that being a victim of physical, sexual, or emotional abuse can also open the door. Doors can be opened by any sin that we have seen or experienced during our lifetime.

The scriptures teach to simply submit to God, resist the devil, and he will run from you (James 4:7). Repenting is submitting our thoughts, mind, and bodies to live for Jesus instead of Satan.

Bruce Greyson and Nancy Bush completed nine years of research on near-death experiences for the International Association of Near Death Studies. The findings were that many who died in the hospital had reported having encounters with demonic beings prior to regaining a heartbeat. They also reported other types of experiences, which we were heavenly and did not include encounters with demonic beings.

Robert Monroe founded the Monroe Institute after having what is known as "out of body experiences" now called OBE's. The institute is located in Faber, Virginia in the United States. Many people throughout the world have been to the programs developed by Monroe to include individuals from France, Germany, Japan, Australia and from other parts of the world. The United States Military and the former Director of the Intelligence and Security Command of the U.S. Army confirmed that the military sent troops to the institute. Monroe was able to leave his body at will and to travel beyond the time-space continuum. Many are aware of the OBE's that people have after they die temporarily in hospitals, but many OBE's occur while people are sound asleep. You may recall feeling as though you had been somewhere before yourself long ago and had what we call a Déjà vu. The U.S Central Intelligence Agency and the National Security Agency utilized his processes in order to train agents to do remote viewing. Monroe devoted an entire chapter in his first book, "Journeys out of the Body" (1972) to his unpleasant encounters with what he called "intelligent animals" that exist in the non-physical realm. He theorized that what he experienced may furnish the basis for demons, goblins, spirits and so on. Monroe also explained in a Journal entry back in 1960 how that rubbery entities attached themselves to his non-physical body. His theologically minded friends had told him to say the Lord's Prayer, but he said that no matter what he did that they stubbornly hung on. Monroe also explained later how a mysterious robed figure came to collect the demons during the out of body experience. Monroe did not give a religious interpretation any of his experiences. The OBE's experienced by Monroe when he was alive with a heartbeat or asleep differed from those experienced by people who had actually died and later returned. One thing is for sure, there is a Devil on the loose that wants your soul. Jesus came to set us free from the bondage to demons while we are on the earth. You must choose to follow Jesus instead of the evil one. The Bible teaches, "Be sober, and vigilant; because your adversary the devil, as a roaring lion, walks about, seeking whom he may devour" (I Peter 5:8). Many who died in the hospital that reported having encounters with demons after clinical death had not previously made a decision to believe Jesus and to repent of sin. Jesus died and rose again for us and that is the good news. We must simply repent and believe the good news. I do not encourage anyone to engage in astral projection or any activity that relates to having a voluntary out of the body experience. Satan can get involved, and he wants to destroy your soul. A lot of people have reported frightening encounters with demons during OBE's after near-death experiences, and there is a danger that you may not return.

If you were to die tonight and returned what would your near-death experience be like? Where would you spend eternity if you did not make it back? We will all one day receive rewards or punishments in the next life. You cannot follow both Jesus and the Devil. No man can serve two masters (Matt. 6:24). The time has come for you to make a very important decision in your life. Heaven and Hell are very real places. Satan is also real and his demons are on the loose and want to influence your mind and live or operate inside of you. It does matter how we live our life upon the earth and what choices we make each day. The false pastors who spoke lies are in Hell. The Bible says in Revelation 21:8-9, "He that overcomes shall inherit all things; and I will be his God, and he shall be my son. But the fearful, and the unbelieving, and the abominable, and murderers, and whoremongers, and sorcerers, and idolaters, and all liars, shall have their part in the lake which burns with fire and brimstone: which is the second death". Jesus warned us, "And fear not them which kill the body, but are not able to kill the soul: but rather fear him which is able to destroy both soul and body in hell" (Matt. 10:28). The Bible says in Revelation 20:10, "The Devil that deceived them was cast into the lake of fire and brimstone, where the beast and the false prophet are, and shall be tormented day and night forever and ever." Don't be tricked. Hell is real and the Devil has tricked men and women out of their souls. We can overcome Satan's trap with help from Jesus. Jesus is the savior. Call on his name. Cry to him for help and deliverance. Get prayer and seek deliverance from The Devil inside. The Bible says, "And whoever was not found written in the Book of Life was cast into the lake of fire" (Rev. 20:15).

Where would you spend eternity if you were to die today? Are you on your way to heaven or on your way to hell? "Strive to enter in at the straight gate: for many, I say unto you, will seek to enter in, and shall not be able" (Luke 13:24). "Not everyone that says Lord, Lord, shall enter into the kingdom of heaven; but he that does the will of my Father in heaven. Many will say in that day, Lord, Lord, have we not prophesied in thy name? And in thy name cast out devils? And in thy name done many wonderful works? And then I will profess to them, I never knew you; depart from me, ye that work iniquity" (Matt. 7:21-23). The Bible says, "And many false prophets shall arise and deceive many" (Matt. 24:11). Look how many false prophets have walked the face of this planet to start a religious movement since Jesus Christ rose from the dead in 33 A.D. Jesus foretold of these events centuries before it happened and said, "For there shall arise false Christs, and false prophets, and shall show great signs and wonders; insomuch that, if it were possible, they shall deceive the very elect" (Matt. 24:24). "Beware of the false prophets that come to you in sheep's clothing, but inwardly they are ravening wolves" (Matt. 7:15). "You shall have no other gods but Jesus" (Exod. 20:4). Repent. "You shall not take the name of the Lord in vain" (Exod. 20:7). Repent. "You shall work for six days and rest on the seventh" (Exod. 20:9-10). Repent. "Honor your father and your mother" (Exod. 20:12). Repent. "Do not kill" (Exod. 20:13). Repent. "Thou shall not commit adultery" (Exod. 20:14). Repent. Do not be a false witness against your neighbor and a liar (Exod. 20:16). Repent. Do not lust for and covet your neighbor's wife, house, car, nor anything that belongs to him (Exod. 20:17). Repent. "Let no man deceive you with vain words: for because of these things comes the wrath of God upon the children of disobedience" (Eph. 5:6). "Know ye not that the unrighteous shall not inherit the kingdom of God? Be not deceived: neither fornicators, nor idolaters, nor adulterers, nor effeminate, nor abusers of themselves with mankind, nor thieves, nor covetous, nor drunkards, nor revilers, nor extortions, shall inherit the kingdom of God" (1 Cor. 6:10-11).

Wake up before it's too late. Don't let Satan deceive you any longer. Renounce all association with him and his kingdom. How long can you gamble with the Devil and obey him and let him deceive you? John said, "Little children, let no man deceive you: he that doeth righteousness is righteous, even as he is righteous. He that commits sin is of the devil: for the devil sinneth from the beginning" (1 John 3:7-8). He further elaborates in First John 3:9- 10 and says, "Whoever is born of God doth not commit sin; for his seed remains in him: and he cannot sin, because he is born of God. In this the children of God are manifest, and the children of the devil: whosoever doeth not righteousness is not of God, neither he that loves not his brother." A true Christian can stumble and fall into sin, and he or she can be forgiven (I John 1:9). A true Christian cannot continue to practice sin and live their life as a disobedient sinner. A true Christian can commit a sin, but they cannot continue to practice sin as a regular deliberate routine in their lifestyle. Are you born again? You are born again once you believe the gospel and repent and have been indwelt by the Holy Spirit. Your life is new in Christ after you repent and believe and have been forgiven. The Bible teaches, "If any man be in Christ, he is a new creature and old things have passed away" (2 Corinthians 5:17). A man must be born again to enter into the kingdom of heaven (John 3:5). Jesus is talking about a spiritual rebirth which occurs when one believes the gospel and repents of sin. Demons will be put out of the physical body when a soul is delivered in Jesus' name. The Holy Ghost indwells within him or her and gives them a new spiritual life (Acts 2:38 and I John 4:14- 16). Without Jesus and his empowerment the unbeliever will not be able to have the power to overcome demons and their deceitful operations within the soul. Jesus promised, "You will receive power after that the Holy Spirit has come upon you" (Acts 1:8). The power promised is also the power to cast out devils (Mark 16:17). Satan is a liar and the Father of lies (John 8:44). It should be nothing strange with the description of Satan as being the Father of lies that demons claim to be the ghosts of the dead or intelligent aliens from a distant galaxy.

Chapter Three

Why is There a Hell?

Which Sins will send us there?

Why is there a hell in the first place? Our Bible teaches us that hell was originally prepared for the devil and his angels (Matt. 25:41). God is also a judge. Would a just judge be fair if he let the murderers go free with no punishment because he loves him or her? Look at the damage to children, families, marriages, communities, cities, towns, villages, and nations by the murderer. Let us suppose that he did not sentence them because he loved them. Would that be just and fair to the victims that were harmed or the one who made the law? No. Likewise, God is a just judge and He has to either punish us for our own sins or punish sin by His only Son taking our place at the cross. God can forgive us of our sins if we accept Jesus and surrender our life to Him by repenting of sin and believing the gospel truth that Jesus died in our place to suffer the penalty for our sins and rose again on the third day. God does not forgive if one does not confess sin, repent of sin, and believe and accept the gospel truth that Jesus was sentenced to death for us to give us the free gift of eternal life. "Vengeance is Mine, I will repay, says the Lord" (Rom. 12:19). God will execute judgment upon each unrepentant sinner.

What Sins Can Take Us to Hell?

All sins should be repented of if one wants to go to heaven. Any sin can take us to hell. Jesus said, "Except you repent, ye shall likewise perish" (Luke 13:3). People who are stingy and selfish are described as the goat in God's left hand that will be thrown into everlasting fire, which was prepared for the devil and his angels (Matt. 25:40- 41). The world is full of plenty of people who fail to do what they ought to do with the money, houses, cars, and the prosperity that they have. The Evangelist doesn't have the time to share every sin with the hearer, but it is important that each soul learns what each and every sin is. "People are destroyed due to a lack of knowledge" (Hosea 4:6). Sin is an offense to men on the earth and to God. The preacher must also notify the sinner that all sin must be repented of in order to receive eternal life through Jesus Christ. All sin can take us to hell if we don't repent of it and believe the good news of the gospel of Jesus Christ and obey. If a sinner doesn't know what sin is, then how can he or she repent?

Repentance is godly sorrow from the heart regarding offense towards God, and a change of mind and heart regarding sin. It is when we cry out to God and confess our sins and we ask Him to help us to change. Unless we know what sin is and what to repent of we will be doomed to the lake of fire. The sorcerers who heard the gospel also repented of sorcery and burned their books! In Acts 19:18-20 the Bible says, "And many that believed came, and confessed, and showed their deeds. Many of them also which used curious arts brought their books together, and burned them before all men, and they counted the price of them, and found it fifty thousand pieces of silver." Repent of all sin in your life.

Chapter Four

What are the Sins in the Bible?
And What Must We Must Repent of?

Sin is the transgression of God's law. The Bible says, "Now we know that what things the law saith, it says to them that are under the law: that every mouth may be stopped, and all the world may become guilty before God" (Romans 3:19). Furthermore, the scriptures declare, "As it is written, there is none righteous, no, not one" (Romans 3:10). The Evangelist has the important task of ensuring that the sinner is aware of how he has failed to obey the commands and requirements of God. As long as he or she believes that they are good enough to go to heaven as they are they will see no need for repentance and faith in Jesus Christ. The Bible says, "For all have sinned, and come short of the glory of God" (Romans 3:23). It is crucial for a lost sinner to believe that he cannot earn his way to heaven and that he is not good enough. It is also crucial that a lost sinner recognizes that he is utterly helpless before God to save himself from his sinful condition. He or she must be persuaded that is it not possible for him or her to be brought into a right standing before God on the basis of meritorious works.

Sin is sin and we must repent of sin. Gambling is sin because of covetousness (Luke 12; 15). Fortune telling is sin (Acts 16:16- 18; Deut. 18:10-11). Extortion is obtaining money illegally and it too, is sin (Matt. 23:25; 1 Cor. 6:9). Gluttony is eating too much and it is sin based on (Deut. 21:20; Prov. 23:21). Rejecting Jesus Christ is sin (John 12:48). Lying to the Holy Ghost and keeping back part of what God wants is sin and such was the case with Ananias and Sapphira (Acts 5:3). Being a deceitful worker of Christ is sin (2 Cor. 11:13). Hating God is sin (Rom. 1:30). Hating your brother is sin (1 John 2:11). Carrying a grudge against anyone in your heart is sin (1 Pet. 4:9; James 5:9). Refusing to leave the mother of harlots known as the great harlot is sin (Rev. 18:4; 2 Cor. 6:16- 17). Being a false witness that speaks lies is sin (Prov. 6:16, 19; Matt. 15:19; Exod. 20:16).

Sin is sin. Laziness is sin (2 Thess. 3:10-12; Prov. 6:6-8; Eph. 5:16; Heb. 6:12). Putting your job or work of your own hands before God is sin (Deut. 31:29; Rev. 9:20). Evil thoughts and fantasies is sin (Matt. 15:19; Mark 7:21). Adultery is sin (Exod. 20:14; Matt. 19:18). Not being content with what you do have is sin (Heb. 13:5). Complaining about what you don't have is sin (Num. 11:4-6, 21:5). Wearing the clothing of the opposite sex is sin (Deut. 22:5). Sowing discord by pitting one person against another is sin (Prov. 6:16, 19). Cursing men by saying bad things about them is sin (James 3:9). Coveting the things that belong to others including their house, land, money, or other belongings is sin (Matt. 7:22; Exod. 20:17; Ezek. 33:11). Fornication is sex outside of marriage and is sin (1 Cor. 6:9). Homosexuality is sin.

Sin is still sin. Being with another man as if he was a woman is also sin (Lev. 18:22; Rom. 1:24-28; 1 Cor. 6:9). Jealousy is sin (2 Cor. 12:20; Luke 15:27-31). The Bible says that jealousy is as cruel as the grave. (Song of Solomon 8:6.) Murder is sin (Exod. 20:13; Matt. 19:18). Justifying what wicked people do is sin

(Prov. 17:15). Hiding hatred with lying lips is sin (Prov. 10:18). Making a graven image of anything in heaven or earth is sin (Exod. 20:4, 32:8, 21). All occult activity is sin (Deut. 18:9-14; Lev. 20:6; Isa. 8:19). The occult activity is having your daughter to pass through the fire, divination, observers of times, enchanters, witches, charmers, consultants with familiar spirits, wizards, and necromancers.

Sin is still a sin. Offending the children or little ones by words or deeds is sin (Matt. 18:6: Mark 9:42; Luke 17:2; 1 Cor. 8:9-13). A woman not loving her children is sin (Titus 2:4). Refusing to obey the laws of man is sin (1 Pet. 2:13-15). Being double minded is sin because a double minded man is unstable in all his ways (James 4:7-10). A proud look is sin (Prov. 6:17). Not providing for your own family or children is sin (1 Tim. 5:8). Rape is taking sex by force and it is sin punishable by death (Deut. 22:25-27). It is sin to be called a Rabbi or Master (Matt. 23:8). Loving money is sin (Heb. 13:5; 1 Tim. 6:10). The Bible says that the love of money is the root of all evil. Thinking that you're righteous is sin (Matt. 2:17).

Sin is still a sin. Buying and selling for your own profit in God's church is sin (Mark 11:15). Jesus said that His house is called a house of prayer, but they turned it into a den of thieves. Having sex with a prostitute is sin (1 Cor. 6:15-18). Prostitutes are not just on the streets; there are plenty of call girls that have houses that invite their clients into their homes. Having sex with a relative is a sin (Deut. 27:20-24). Having sex with a virgin and not marrying her is a sin (Deut. 22:28-29). Having sex with a virgin who is engaged is sin (Deut. 22:23-24). A virgin who has sex with someone else she is not engaged to sins if she doesn't cry out and tell others (Deut. 22:23-24).

Sin is still a sin. A rebellious son who disobeys his parents is in sin (Deut. 21:18-21). Rebellion against a parent is a sin punishable by death in the Bible. Provoking your children to anger and wrath is sin (Eph. 6:4). A lot of folks forget that it is sin to provoke someone else to anger and wrath. A soft or gentle answer turns away wrath but grievous words stir up anger (Prov. 15:1). Quarreling and arguing is sin (2 Cor. 12:20). Rebellion against God is sin (Dan. 9:5-9). Rioting is a sin (2 Pet. 2:13). Riotous living is a sin. Being in wrath and having a fit of rage is sin (Gal. 5:20). Ambitions that are entirely selfish are sin (Gal. 5:19- 20). A pastor or shepherd that rules with cruelty is in sin (Ezek. 34:4). A shepherd or pastor that does not feed the flock is in sin (Ezek. 34:8). Knowing to do good and then not doing what we should do is sin (James 4:17).

Sin is still a sin. It is a sin not to be ashamed of your sin (Jer. 8:12). Jeremiah asked, "Were they ashamed when they had committed abomination? No, they were not at all ashamed, neither could they blush: therefore shall they fall among them that fall: in the time of their visitation they shall be cast down, says the Lord" (Jer. 8:12). It is a sin not to confess your sin to God and to man (1 John 1:19; James 5:16; Psalm 32:5; Prov. 28:13). It is sin for a fool to mock sin, and that means to laugh at it and have pleasure in seeing it or talking about it (Prov. 14:9). It is sin to do your own will or to be self-willed if it is not God's will (2 Pet. 2:10). It is sin to entice a nation to sin (1 Kings 14:16). The shepherd or pastor that did not bring again that which was driven away is in sin (Ezek. 34:4). Not paying the taxes you owe is sin (Rom. 13:6-18: Luke 20:25).

Sin is still a sin. Tattling, meddlers, busybodies, and talebearers sin when they tell stories about other people that they may think will hurt them, or they may think is funny (1 Tim. 5:13). A stubborn child of God sins when he refuses to obey his parents in the Lord at the church (Eph. 6:1). A person sins when they are stubborn and refuse to submit to authority and to obey.

(Isa. 48:4-8; 1 Sam. 15:23). There are stubborn children, stubborn wives, stubborn husbands, stubborn workers, stubborn leaders, and stubborn nations. Seeing things with your eyes like television or movies that are contrary to godliness is sin (Ps. 101:3). I will set no wicked thing before mine eyes. Getting a tattoo is sin (Lev. 19:28; Deut. 14:1). Swearing is sin (Jer. 23:10). Stealing is sin (Exod. 20:15; Mark 7:22).

Sin is still a sin. Refusing to admit you are a sinner is a sin (Jer. 8:6; 1 John 1:8). Saying you have not sinned is a sin (1 John 1:10). Slandering people by saying things to ruin their reputation or other mean and hateful things is sin, and is also called slander or backbiting (Mark 7:20-23; Rom. 1:30; 2 Cor. 12:10). Being a traitor is sin (2 Tim. 3, 4; Luke 6:16). Calling that which is evil good and good evil is sin, which brings judgment upon the one who does it or upon the entire nation (Isa. 5:20). Worrying about tomorrow is sin (Matt. 6:34). The tongue is a world of sin (James 3:3-13). Speaking words of hatred with the tongue is sin (Ps. 109:3). Cursing those that hate you is also sin (Matt. 5:44). Making your own belly your God is sin (Phil. 3:19). Not giving thanks to God in all of your circumstances is sin (1 Thess. 5:18; Rom. 1:21).

Sin is still a sin. Not giving tithes and offerings is sin (Mal. 3:8- 9; Lev. 27:32; Deut. 14:22). Yielding the members of your body to sinful desires is sin (Rom. 6:13). Teaching any doctrine that is not in the Bible is heresy and that is sin (1 Tim. 1:3). Being a witch or having anything to do with a witch is sin (Deut. 18:10- 11). Making a vow and not keeping it is sin (Eccl. 5:4- 6). Being a violent man or doing violent deeds is sin (Ps. 18:48; Luke 3:14; Ezek. 8:17). Being an unjust steward and disloyalty with what belongs to another is sin (Luke 16:10, 12). Not being content with your wages is sin (Luke 3:14; Matt. 20:1- 6). Paying unfair wages is sin (James 5:14). Being wise in your own eyes is sin (Isa. 5:21). Wives who do not submit to their own husbands are in sin (Eph. 5:22).

Sin is still a sin. Adding to or taking away from the Word of God and prophecy is sin (Rev. 22:18-19). Not turning away from a false science that contradicts God's Word is sin (1 Tim. 6:20). Being stiff-necked towards God's Word is sin (Acts 7:1). Corrupting the Word of God is sin (2 Cor. 2:17). Despising the Word of God is sin (Is. 5:24; Num. 15:30). Disobeying the Word of God is sin (1 John 3:4). Handling God's Word deceitfully is sin (2 Cor. 4:2). Not hiding the Word of God in your heart is sin (Ps. 119:11). Not reading the Word of God daily is sin (Ps. 1:2; Acts 17:11; 1 Pet. 2:2). Not teaching God's Word to your children is sin (Deut. 6:7). Stopping your ears from hearing God's Word is sin (Acts 7:57). Not studying God's Word is sin (Prov. 3:3; 2 Tim. 2:15). Being ungrateful is sin (2 Tim. 3:1).

Sin is sin. Hating instruction is sin (Ps. 50:17). Loving this world of which Satan is the god of (little "g" as he is not Almighty as is God) and the things that are in this world, including material things is sin (1 John 2:15-17). Being friends with this world makes us the enemy of God and is sin (James 4:4). Staying mad and letting the sun go down on your wrath is sin (Eph. 4:26). Getting entangled with the affairs of this life on earth is sin (2 Tim. 2:4). Conforming to this world in dress, speech, thoughts, ways, attitudes, beliefs and values is sin (Rom. 12:2). Not acknowledging thine iniquity is sin (Jer. 3:13). Being ashamed of Jesus and His words is sin (Mark 8:38). Blasphemy against the Holy Spirit is sin (Mark 3:29). Not clothing children that need clothing is sin (Matt. 25:43). Not feeding children that are hungry is sin (Matt. 25:43).

Sin is still a sin. Not visiting God's children that are sick is a sin (Matt. 25:43). Not visiting God's children that are in prison is sin (Matt. 25:43). Hindering or beating a servant of God is sin

(Luke 12:45). Despising one of God's children is sin (Matt. 18:10). Bitterness in the heart against another because we have not forgiven them is sin (Acts 8:23; Rom. 3:14; Eph. 4:31; Heb. 12:15). Assaulting others physically is sin (Exod. 21:18-19; Acts 14:5). Being afraid to confess Jesus to people is sin (John 14:12). Abortion is sin (Exod. 21:22; Jer. 1:4-5). Not abstaining from all the appearances of evil is sin (1 Thess. 5:22). Going to the church of the mother of harlots is sin (Rev. 17:5; 18:4-5). Not bringing your children up in the training and instruction of the Lord is sin (Eph. 6:4). Not spanking a disobedient child is sin (Prov. 13:24).

Sin is still a sin. Forsaking church attendance when the believers are assembling themselves together is sin (Heb. 10:25; Acts 2:46; Eccl. 4:9-12). Not becoming as a little child before God and humbling yourself is sin (Matt. 18:3). Speaking evil things about your brother in Christ is sin (James 4:1). Breaking up homes is sin; putting asunder what God has joined together (Matt. 19:6). Being a busybody and meddling in someone else's matters is sin (Prov. 20:13; 1 Tim. 5:13). Not paying what you owe is sin (Matt. 5:26). Making bad debts is sin (Rom. 13:8). Cursing the Lord's name is sin (Exod. 20:7). Seeing counsel that is not from God is sin (Isa. 30:1; Ps. 1:1-4). Not being meek and quiet is sin (1 Pet. 3:4). Drug use is known as sorcery and that is sin (Rev. 9:21). Getting drunk is called drunkenness in the Bible and this is sin (Luke 12:45; Rom. 13:13; 1 Cor. 6:10).

Sin is still a sin. Turning to false counsel and fables is sin (2 Tim. 4:4). Despising those that are good is sin (2 Tim. 3:1-3). Having contentions towards others' strife is also sin (Prov. 17:4). Divorce, except for immorality or fornication by a spouse is sin (Matt. 19:9). Being discontent with what you have is sin (Phil. 4:11; 1 Tim. 6:8; Luke 3:14). Defrauding others is sin (James 5:14; Ps. 10:7; 1 Thess. 4:6). Finding fault with others is sin (Jude 16). Flattering others for personal gain is sin (Jude 16; Prov. 26:28).

Circulating a false report is sin (Exod. 23:1). Calling a man your
Father upon the earth is sin (Matt. 23:9). Using false scales or
balances when making a decision is sin (Prov. 11:1). Not doing
everything you do as unto the Lord is sin (Col. 3:23). Not loving
God with all your heart, soul, and mind is sin (Matt. 22:37).

Sin is still sin. Hardening your heart from God is also sin
(Heb. 13:8). Denying that Jesus is God in the flesh is sin (John 1:14;
1 John 4:3). Denying that Jesus is the King of Kings and Lord
of Lord's is sin (Rev. 19:6). Denying that Jesus Christ created all
things is sin (John 1:3; Heb. 1:1-2; Col. 1:14-17). Denying that Jesus Christ was raised from the dead is sin (Rom. 10:9). Whoever
shall keep the whole law and offend at any point is guilty of sin
(James 2:10). Greediness is sin (Eph. 4:19; Col. 3:5). Not hating
the works of them that turn from God is sin (Ps. 101:3). Not
setting your heart on things above but on earthly things of the
world is sin (Col. 3:2). Working wickedness in your own heart
is sin (Ps. 58:2). Refusing to honor your father and your mother
is sin (Exod. 20:12). Professing to be saved but denying God in
your works is sin (Titus 1:6).

Sin is still sin. Refusing to follow after and pursue a life of
holiness is sin (Heb. 12:14). It is sin to say that we are Christians
if we don't keep His commandments (1 John 2:4). It is sin to draw
near to God or to honor Him with words, but not with your heart
(Matt. 15:8). It is sin to trust in your own ways and not God's
ways (Hosea. 10:13; Prov. 3:5-7). Listening to the voice of your
spouse instead of the voice of God is sin (Gen. 3:17). Interfer-
ing or hindering those who wish to be saved is sin (Luke 11:52).
Worshiping angels rather than God is sin (Col. 2:18). Kidnap-
ping a child is sin (Exod. 21:16). Not being kind to others is sin
(Col. 3:12). Bringing a graven image into your home is a sin
(Deut. 7:25-26). Offending others by what you say or do is sin
(James 3:2; Matt. 18:6; Luke 17:2). It is sin to be effeminate and

for a male to act like a female (1 Cor. 6:9).

Sin is still sin. It is sin to refuse to give to the poor (Prov. 28:27; Luke 18:2, 19:8). The prayer of the wicked is sin (Ps. 109:7). Praying with selfish motives to consume what you get with your own lusts is sin (James 4:3). Being prayer-less, or not having a life of prayer is sin (1 Thess. 5:17; 1 Sam. 12:23). Making a long prayer to be seen of men is sin (Mark 12:40). Regarding iniquity in the heart causes God not to hear our prayers and is sin (Ps. 66:18). Departing from a church and a preacher because they teach the uncompromising Word of God is sin (John 6:60; 2 Tim. 4:3- 4, 10). Going to preachers who don't teach sound doctrine but tell you what you want to hear is sin (2 Tim. 4:3). Being a false pastor or a false minister is sin (2 Cor. 11:13-15). Preaching to please men is sin (1 Thess. 2:4-6). Preaching after the traditions of men is sin (1 Cor. 2:13).

Sin is sin. Preaching with philosophy and vain deceit is sin (Col. 2:4, 8). It is sin to let a false prophet or teacher prophesy or teach (Rev. 2:20). Preaching to get the glory of men is sin (1 Thess. 2:4-6). Preaching doctrines other than the Bible is sin (1 Tim. 1:3-4, 6). Refusing to pray in the name of Jesus is sin (John 14:13). Smoking is sin (Rom. 12:1; 13:14; 1 Cor. 3:16-18). A person sins when they do not strive to enter into heaven by not watching and not praying to be accounted worthy to enter into heaven (Luke 21:36). We sin by having traditions of men that take the place of God's will and His commandments (Matt. 15:3). Trusting in ourselves instead of God is sin (2 Cor. 1:9). A man who will not work is in sin (2 Thess. 3:10). Look at the damage that laziness has caused in this nation alone. Worldly mindedness is sin (Rom. 8:5-7).

Sin is sin. It is sin when the younger people will not submit themselves to their elders (1 Pet. 5:5). Not restraining the tongue is sin (James 1:26). Thinking evil in your heart about God's children is sin (Matt. 9:4). Putting a stumbling block in the path of God's children to attempt to ensnare one or all of them into a sin is sinful (Acts 15:1; Rom. 14:13). Women sin in vile affections when they lust after other women and turn the natural use of the body against nature. (Rom. 1:26) Deceiving your neighbor is a sin (Jer. 9:5-6). Believing in evolution is a sin (Ps. 100:3). Trusting in lies is sin (Jer. 7:4). Overindulgence is sin (Luke 21:34). Causing a weak brother to stumble is sin (1 Cor. 8:11). Playing favorites and being partial to some is sin (James 2:1-5). Being halfhearted and neither hot nor cold but lukewarm towards God is sin (Rev. 3:16). Loving in word or tongue by not in deed and truth is sin (1 John 3:18).

Sin is still a sin. A lady who is not dressed in modest apparel is in sin (1 Tim. 2:9; Prov. 7:10). Having a covetous and unquenchable desire to gain things of the world including houses and material things is sin (Hab. 2:9). Envy in the heart because of the success of others is also sin (1 Tim. 6:4; Acts 13:45; Rom. 1:29). Making up excuses as to why you can't follow Jesus now is sin (Luke 14:18-24). Having any god that comes before God Almighty is sin (Exod. 20:3; Ps. 81:9; Acts 15:20). Forsaking God is sin (Jer. 16:11). Talking against God is sin against God (Jude 15). Refusing to forsake everything to follow Jesus is sin (Luke 14:33). Failure to give God the glory is sin (Luke 17:7; Rom. 1:21; Acts 12:23). Not receiving the man of God who was sent by God is a sin (Luke 9:5).

Sin is still sin. A servant who does not use the talent or gift that God gives him sins and is a slothful servant (Matt. 25:24- 40). Robbing God by not giving 10% of your income is sin (Mal. 3:8- 9). Thinking that godliness is the way to financial gain is sin (1 Tim. 6:5). Trusting in riches is sin (Ps. 52:7). Being in pursuit of your heart's own desires and not God's is sinful (Phil. 2:21). Giving honor to men as a god is sin (Act 14:11-18). Failing to teach judgment, mercy, and faith is sin for those in churches who teach others (Matt. 23:23). Impatience is sin (Luke 21:19; Heb. 10:36). A person sins when they don't help the poor and needy (Ezek. 16:49). They are cursed when they don't give to the poor (Prov. 28:27). Being a lover of pleasure more than a lover of God is sin (2 Tim. 3:4). Judging your brother in Christ is a sin (Matt. 7:1-3).

Sin is still sin. One sins by not giving thanks to God in all things because the circumstances are the will of God concerning them (1 Thess. 5:18). Having malice and ill will toward others is sin (Matt. 7:22; Rom. 1:29). Feet that are swift to run and do mischief is an abomination and is sin (Prov. 6:18). Refusing to give to those with a need when they ask if you have it to give is sin (Matt. 5:42). A person who is not perfect is in sin because of the command of Jesus to be perfect (Matt. 5:48). Coming near the door of a prostitute's door is sin (Prov. 5:8). Lusting after the beauty of a strange woman in the heart is sin (Prov. 6:25). Coming to the house of a whore is sin and the way to hell (Prov. 7:27). Wine is a mocker and whoever is deceived by it is in sin (Prov. 20:1).

Sin is still sin. A woman who has a heart full of snares and nets to trap men gives her lover an experience more bitter than death and this is sin (Eccl. 7:26). Looking upon a woman with lust in the eyes is adultery in the heart and this is sin (Matt. 5:28). Seeking the material things of this world from God before seeking His kingdom and His righteousness first is sin (Matt. 6:33). Refusing to forgive others of their trespasses against you means that God won't forgive you and this is sin (Matt. 5:15). Professing to love God while hating a brother in Christ makes one a liar and this is sin (1 John 4:20). He who loves God loves his brother also (1 John 4:21). Whoever hates his brother is a murderer and has no eternal life in him, which is sin (1 John 3:15). Murmuring and complaining is sin (Jude 16; Phil. 1:14).

Sin is still sin. Filthy dreamers who defile the flesh, despise dominion, and speak evil of authorities are in sin (Jude 8). Having a form of godliness but denying the power thereof is sin, and saints are told to turn away from such things (2 Tim. 3:6). Evil men and seducers who deceive others and who have been deceived are in sin (2 Tim. 3:13). Having no natural affection toward the opposite sex, being a false accuser, being fierce, incontinent, and a despiser of those that are good are all sins (2 Tim. 3:3). Turning your ears away from the truth to hear fables is sin (2 Tim. 4:4). Refusing to hear sound doctrine and chasing teachers who tickle their itching ears due to your own lusts is sin (2 Tim. 4:3). Being a false pastor and subverting houses, teaching things you ought not to teach for filthy lucre, which is money, is sin (Titus 1:11).

Sin is sin. All unrighteousness is sin (1 John 5:17). Drinking from the cup of the Lord and from the cup of devils is sin (1 Cor. 10:21). Being unequally yoked together in a relationship with unbelievers is sin (2 Cor. 6:14). Not coming out from among the sinners and living a sanctified and separate life, and not being separate is sin (2 Cor. 6:17). You are not to keep company, if any man that is called a brother (in the Lord) be a fornicator, or covetous, or an idolater, or a railer, or a drunkard, or an extortion; with such a one no not to eat for this is sin (1 Cor. 5:9-11). Knowing the way of righteousness and turning from the holy commandment delivered unto you is sin (2 Pet. 2:21). The Word of God describes it as the dog turning to his own vomit again and the pig that was washed to her wallowing in the mire (2 Pet. 2:22).

Sin is still sin. A teacher or preacher who does not teach and preach the truth has brought in damnable heresies and destruction to themselves, and he or she is in sin (2 Pet. 2:1). The pastor that forsakes the right way and runs like the prophet Balaam into pulpits as a hireling for money is in sin (2 Pet. 2:15). The love of the things of this world and the lust for things in the eyes with the passion of lust in the flesh and the egocentric pride of this life is not of God but of this world and is also sin (1 John 2:15-16). A whoremonger and an adulterer God will judge because this is sin (Heb. 13:4). The very motion of lust and want and desire of covetousness within the flesh is sin (Rom. 7:7). Having pleasure or being entertained by them who commit things worthy of death is sin (Rom. 1:32). Departing from the faith to give heed to seducing spirits and doctrines of devils is sin (1 Tim. 4:1).

Sin is still sin. Receiving the mark of the beast on your right hand or your forehead in order to buy or sell is sin (Rev. 13:16-17). The mark is the number of a man, it is 666 (Rev. 13:18). Refusing to confess your faults one to another that you may be healed is sin and a cover up (James 5:16). Not submitting to every ordinance of man for the Lord's sake is sin. Whether it be to the king as supreme or unto governors, as unto them that are sent by him for the punishment of evildoers, and for the praise of them that do well (1 Pet. 2:13). Not being holy because God is holy is a sin (1 Pet. 1:16). If we say we have no sin, we deceive ourselves, and the truth is not in us (1 John 1:8). There is not a just man upon the earth that doeth good and sinneth not (Eccl. 7:20). As it is written, There is none righteous, no, not one (Rom. 3:10).

The good news is that Jesus Christ died for all of your sins and rose again from the dead on the third day. You are not guilty of sin anymore if you repent and believe he died in your place and nailed your sin to the cross. We must repent of sin to God. He nailed your guilty record of sin to the cross and you are forgiven once you truly repent within your heart and believe the good news. Jesus will then set you free from sin. Jesus can deliver your mind, thoughts, and ways from bondage to Satan the Devil. He loves you and died to save you from the flames of hell and to set you free from bondage to all demons that desire to hold you in spiritual bondage and enslavement to sin. Be set free.

Chapter Five

Who on Earth Burns in Hell?

Witches of Witchcraft

The religion known as Wicca is the modern day religion of Witchcraft. A few hundred years ago Matthew Douglas started the witch hunts in Germany where witches were put to death. If anyone found a witch they would be executed if proven guilty after they were given a trial. Nearly one hundred thousand witches were put to death during the witch-hunts in Germany between 1600 and 1700 A.D. Today witchcraft is legal in America and the church and School of Wicca is located in New Bern, North Carolina. We now also have chaplains who are witches that work as professionals in many of our prisons. Psychics are in touch with demons and books are everywhere in bookstores about how to cast a spell and what to do to become a witch. Withes are in the military.

Television shows such as Charmed and books such as Harry Potter have seduced the minds of children and teenagers, and have hoodwinked them into exploring the supernatural. We see magicians levitating online and performing miracles that are scientifically impossible. On television talk shows you can find people who are necromancers who are in touch with the spirits that claim to communicate with the dead. All of these things and more were done during biblical days, and God has His own indictment against it. God Almighty said, "There shall not be found among you any one that makes his son or daughter to pass through the fire, or that uses divination, or an observer of times, or an enchanter, or a witch, or a charmer, or a consulter with familiar spirits, or a wizard, or a necromancer. For all that do these things are an abomination unto the Lord: and because of these abominations the Lord thy God doth drive them out before thee" (Deut. 18:10-13). In Exodus 22:18 the Bible also says, "Thou shalt not suffer a witch to live," and that all sorcerers shall have their part in the lake that burns with fire and brimstone in Revelation 21:8.

Hell is the end for the witch and the magician with the sorcerer, necromancer, and wizard. Repent of all these sins and ask God to forgive you. God loves you and does not want to see your soul eternally damned in the lake of fire and brimstone. Believe that Jesus is the only true God and that He died for your sins on the cross and rose again. Repent and turn away from these sins and stop them once and for all, or you will surely perish in the flames of hell below. Jesus is the Almighty God and He rose again from the dead on the third day. The witches and sorcerers who repented during biblical days also burned their books. The Bible says, "And many that believed came, and confessed, and showed their deeds. Many of them also which used curious arts brought their books together, and burned them before all men, and they counted the price of them, and found it fifty thousand pieces of silver" (Acts 19:18-20).

Homosexuals

Many pastors and preachers throughout the world have been promoting or staying silent on the issue of same sex marriage and equal rights in civil unions in situations where couples are gay. You have seen by reading the story of the destruction of Sodom that

Sodom and Gomorrah were destroyed by fire and brimstone because of homosexuality. Others' sins were also prevalent in the cities that the archaeologists identified. More and more bishops and
members of the clergy are now professing to be openly gay or not
opposed to same sex marriage, or same sex couples. We are now
living in a society where some pastors and Christian musicians are
openly gay. Are they truly God's children, or do they belong to the
Devil? I am also aware that laws have been passed regarding hate
crimes against these groups. A Christian can love these people but
they have to hate the sin that God hates, but not hate the people. I
find it very disturbing that so many actors in Hollywood that are
men are so easily manipulated to play in roles in which they have
to act like a homosexual when they are supposedly not.

In 2012, President Barack Obama mentioned it publicly that
he now supports gay marriages. We also have many senators, con-
gressman, and governors who support an amendment to the con-
stitution to redefine what constitutes a marriage. WAKE UP! This
is Bible prophecy everyone. Jesus spoke of His return to the earth
and He specifically said that it would be just as it was during the
days of Sodom and Gomorrah. During Sodom the men tried to
break into Lot's house to get to the angels who looked like men.
They had their own agenda. God destroyed these cities by fire and
brimstone that fell from the sky. Homosexuality is still a sin. It is in
fact an abomination. God said, "Thou shalt not lie with mankind as
with womankind: it is abomination" in Leviticus 18:22. The Bible
says in Revelation 21:8 that the abominable shall have their part in
the lake that burns with fire and brimstone. Yes, dear friends, God
loves those that are gay and He died for their sins too, but He wants
them to repent of these abominations and to turn to Jesus for salvation. No person who is a practicing homosexual can enter into
heaven and are eternally doomed to the lake of fire, based on Revelation 21:8. The fact that people have endorsed it does not mean

that Jesus approves of it. Jesus is not a politician and the wrath of God is eternal hell. Repent of all homosexuality and turn to Jesus in faith and trust Him for your salvation. God loves you and does not want you to burn in the fires of hell below. He can forgive you but He wants you to admit that homosexuality is sin and ask him to save you from your sins. Once a person dies and goes straight to hell, they are eternally damned. There then is no way out.

The Bible says, "For this cause God gave them up unto vile affections: for even their women did change the natural use into that which is against nature. And likewise the men, leaving the natural use of the woman, burned in their own lust one toward another, men with men working that which is unseemly, and receiving in themselves that recompense of their error which was meet. And even as they did not like to retain God in their knowledge, God gave them over to a reprobate mind, to do those things, which are not convenient. (The phrase "reprobate mind" is found in Rom. 1:28 in reference to those whom God has rejected as godless and wicked. They "suppress the truth by their wickedness," and it is upon these people that the wrath of God rests. (See Rom. 1:18.) Being filled with unrighteousness, fornication, wickedness, covetousness, maliciousness; full of envy, murder, debate, deceit, malignity; whisperers, backbiters, haters of God, despiteful, proud, boasters, inventors of evil things, disobedient to parents, without understanding, covenant breakers, without natural affection, implacable, unmerciful. Who knowing the judgment of God, that they which commit such things are worthy of death, not only do the same, but have pleasure in them that do them" (Rom. 1:26-32).

Idolaters

In this life, people are often in a greater pursuit of relationships with people including friends and family members than a relationship with Jesus. We often chase and prioritize material things such as cars, houses, land, and material possessions. People worship the dollar, businesses, careers, fame, wealth, music, and even people. Sports figures, movie stars, musicians, politicians, and even popular inspirational public speakers in churches have been turned into little gods or idols. Secular educational universities and philosophies including many sciences and worldly systems of knowledge, science, and religions have been turned into gods. Psychology is an idol that is worshiped and has replaced Bible, theology, God, and Christianity in terms of what people are turning to for problems within the soul. Many of these things are not evil, but are worshiped and prioritized ahead of God, which makes them idols. People turn to psychotherapists before Jesus and to drugs before God. They celebrate sports figures and glorify knowledge, which is worldly, secular and misleading. They worship themselves and the work of their own hands, and their many accomplishments and achievements upon the earth. No idolater shall inherit the kingdom of God (1 Cor. 6:9). Thou shall have no other gods before me (Exod. 20:3). The Bible says to love not the world, neither the things that are in the world because the lust of the eyes, lust of the flesh, and the pride of life are not of God but of this world (1 John 2:15-17).

Prostitutes

Studies show that some women prostitute to support a drug habit, but this is not always the case. Sometimes the pimps search for and find young and vulnerable runaway girls who grew up needy and lacked attention and affection from a father. Pimps may sometimes flatter them and take their virginity away by providing them with both attention and a sense of security. They may give them money after they introduce them to prostitution to reinforce the need in them to feel secure, while paying them attention and acting as a protector all at the same time. It then becomes a learned behavior; a form of enslavement to a trade because of money, and an emotional trap as well. However, not all girls come into this trade because a pimp turned them into a prostitute. Many people think that it is simply to get paid and to make money.

The lack of money is a motive for prostitution. It is true that many girls get into it due to desperation when cash is running low, while they are either in college or have a financial crisis. Some have boyfriends just to pay the bills or even marry because they know the man has good money, or that he will help them get their bills paid. You have people who believe that the girls who prostitute were sexually abused as a child, and that they consequently grew up seeing themselves as an object to gratify the needs of a man. It is true that from a statistical standpoint, that a large number of sexual abuse victims do become prostitutes, such as the transvestites and others, but not all prostitutes are victims of sexual abuse. Some girls are desperate and homeless and have no family to turn to for financial support. They know that selling their bodies is a way to get fast cash.

Prostitution can also be simply a learned behavior. It is true that some girls get caught up into prostitution because they had friends or relatives that they learned the behavior from. People who have studied the mind say that it is a combination of sexual addiction and the need for financial support from a man. However, it is still a behavior that is learned.

Experts say that the constant need for revalidation from a man due to low self-esteem issues is also a major factor in most cases of prostitution. After all, if someone is paying a girl, it must mean that the man thinks they are a knockout, and for many girls, who are divorced, rejected, or feeling unloved, this is an immediate drug in terms of revalidating their poor self-image and boosting their feelings of worth. They can learn to medicate self-image by observing others. Some psychologists say that it is a result of sex addiction first, meaning this lady turns to sex to medicate her self-image. The idea is that after turning to sex to medicate hurts by validating oneself and the self-esteem, sex addiction often combines with co-dependency which is the need to be needed by a man and the need to feel secure both financially and emotionally. They may see themselves as both a sex addict out of control and as a codependent needing to latch on to men for validation and financial support. They are emotionally vulnerable and weak. The addict may do it for the validation of their self-image, but the co-dependent is driven by the need to be needed, and the need to feel secure financially. Marriage is designed to satisfy needs of the sexes in the bible. The woman's need to feel loved and the need to feel secure and provided for financially and this is what marriage was designed for. It was also designed for a man to have his sexual needs met within a marriage and for procreation. Prostitution competes directly with marriage by pulling men and women into activities, which contradict God's whole purpose, plan and design of relationships, sex, and marriage.

Men should stay away from the harlot and married women play. The love of money is the root of all evil (1 Tim. 6:10). We are told to love not the world, neither the things that are in the world. If any man loves the world the love of the Father is not in him. All that is in the world, the lust of the flesh, and the lust of the eyes, and the pride of life is not of the father, but of the world (1 John 2:15-16). The Devil is called the god of this world who has blinded the minds of them that believe not (2 Cor. 4:34). He is called the prince of the power of the air and the spirit, which is at work in the children of disobedience (Eph. 2:2). The Bible says, "For the lips of a strange woman drop as a honeycomb, and her mouth is smoother than oil: But her end is bitter as wormwood, sharp as a two-edged sword. Her feet go down to death; her steps take hold on hell" (Prov. 5:3-5). The Bible says, "Her house is the way to hell, going down to the chambers of death" (Prob. 7:27). The Bible says, "Stolen waters are sweet, and bread eaten in secret is pleasant, but he knows not that the dead are there; and her guests are in the depths of hell" (Prov. 9:17-18). The scriptures also say, "But whoso commit adultery with a woman lacks understanding: he that does it destroys his own soul" (Prov. 6:32). The verse I just quoted is the only verse in the Bible that says that one destroys his very own soul by committing a specific sin. "Lust not after her beauty in your heart, neither let her take you with her eyelids. For by means of a whorish woman is a man brought to a piece of bread: and the adulteress will hunt for the precious life" (Prov. 6:25-26). The Bible says again in Proverbs, "Remove thy way far from her, and come not nigh the door of her house" (Prov. 5:8). "Whoremongers shall have their part in the lake of fire and brimstone". (Rev. 21:8) (A whoremonger is a customer of a prostitute.) Finally, your Bible says, "For this ye know, that no whoremonger, nor unclean person, nor covetous man, who is an idolater, hath any inheritance in the kingdom of Christ and of God. Let no man deceive you with vain words; for because of these things comes the wrath of God upon the children of disobedience" (Eph. 5:5-6).

Chapter Six

Is There Anybody Good Enough to Go to Heaven?

If you were to die tonight, are you sure that you would go to heaven and that you have eternal life? What will you say to God when you stand before him about your life and what would you profess to Him is the reason that you should not go to hell?

Some may say, "I was a good person." Others may say, "I've done more good than bad." Some others may say, "I was not as bad as other people." God's verdict about all of mankind is final. "There is none righteous, no, not one" (Rom. 3:10). "All have sinned and come short of the glory of God". (Rom. 3:23).

We are all as an unclean thing, and all of our righteousness is like filthy rags when God sees us according to Isaiah 64 in the Bible. Jesus said, "…There is none good but one: That is God…" (Matt. 19:17). No one can climb a ladder to heaven because they are good enough to go there. No one can have enough goodness that outweighs the bad to find favor with God. Comparing ourselves to others and saying, "I'm not as bad as others," is not good enough because God still knows about our sins and that we deserve hell. That includes everyone on this planet including church people. God's laws require perfection and perfection was commanded by Jesus in Matthew 5:48. Nobody meets the requirements. Romans 3:19 says, "The law of God causes every mouth to be stopped, and the whole world to stand guilty before God." Nobody can boast.

The good news is that Jesus saves from hell's wrath to come. Jesus came to the world to die for and pay the penalty for our sins to God and he rose on the third day. The Bible says, "For God so loved the world that He gave His only begotten Son that whosoever believes in Him should not perish, but have everlasting life" (John 3:16). If you want Jesus to save you from hell's penalty, confess your sins to Jesus and admit that you are a sinner. Believe that Jesus is the Son of God and that He died for your sins. The Bible says in Second Corinthians 5:21, "God made Him that knew no sin to be sin for us, so that in Him we might become the righteousness of God in Him." God made Jesus guilty of our sins and punished Him in our place. Jesus led the perfect life that we could not live, and God credited His perfection to our record. Jesus died the death that we deserved, and God credited His death as the full payment for all of our sins. You must confess your sins to God, believe in what Christ has done for you, and trust Jesus to save you. Repent of your sins by turning away from them and forsaking them, and accept Jesus in your heart and life as both your Savior and Lord to rule your life. Pray and ask God to direct your path as to what church to visit and where to hear the Word of God preached. All of the believers had all things in common and believed the same doctrine in the early church when it began.

The church started on the day of Pentecost in the second chapter of the historical book of the Acts of the Apostles when all believers were in one place in one accord, and received the promised gift of the Holy Ghost. The Bible says in Acts 2:42, "They continued steadfastly in the Apostles' Doctrine and fellowship, and in the breaking of bread, and in prayers." If possible, attend where the same doctrine is preached and taught that was taught by the earliest apostles during Biblical times. Many false doctrines and false churches have been planted since. Jesus said, "Many false prophets shall arise and deceive many."

So, take heed what you hear and don't just believe anyone that claims to be a preacher. Everything they teach *must* line up with what is written in the Bible.

Sadly, not everyone will go to heaven. Some will be eternally lost. Let us take a look at scientific proof of the reality of hell, what God says about it, and who on the earth may be going there.

Is There a Hell? A Second Look

In a Finland newspaper an article appeared that revealed that a team of geologists and researchers recorded the screams and cries of the damned. Dr. Azzacove, the lead geologist said, "As a communist I don't believe in heaven or the Bible, but as a scientist, I now believe in hell. We are absolutely certain that we drilled through the gates of hell! The drill suddenly began to rotate wildly, indicating that we had reached a large empty pocket or cavern. Temperature sensors showed a dramatic increase in heat to 2,000 degrees Fahrenheit. We lowered a microphone designed to detect the sounds of plate movements down the shaft, but instead of plate movements, we heard a human voice screaming in pain! At first we thought it was our own equipment. But when we made adjustments, our worst suspicions were confirmed. The screams weren't those of a single human, they were the screams and cries of millions."

I want to say at this point that geologists do not need to prove that hell is real. It is real because Jesus said it is real. Don't be fooled. Jesus said, "And fear not them which kill the body, but are not able to kill the soul: but rather fear him which is able to destroy body and soul in hell" (Matt. 10:28). The historical proof of the resurrection of Jesus, which we will discuss in that chapter, proves that everything else Jesus said was fact. The empty tomb Jesus Christ on the 3rd day was too notorious to be denied. He said he would rise long before he was crucified and he has warned us about hell.

The prophet Amos said in the Bible in Amos 9:2 that, "… they dig into hell…" The Bible teaches that hell is beneath the earth and this was taught thousands of years before scientists discovered that the center of the earth was composed of fire and brimstone and called it the core. It's the same sulfur and fire that comes pouring out of volcanoes. In the Book of Numbers chapter 16, God opened up the earth to swallow a group of people straight into hell's pit.

Hell is directly beneath your feet. It is closer to most people than the nearest train station or airport. You must admit to God that you are a sinner, repent and turn away from your sins, believe that Jesus died for your sins to pay the penalty, and that he rose from the dead. You must ask Jesus to save your soul from hell's certainty. Repent and turn from sin and to Jesus and surrender your mind, body, and soul to him.

Many people have had near death experiences and have come back to life after regaining a heartbeat. Many years ago, Dr. Maurice Rawlings, a specialist in internal medicine and an atheist considered all faith and Christianity as a fraud. But in 1977 he was resuscitating a man who was terrified and screaming, and he was going down into the flames of hell. He said in his book and I quote, "Each time he regained a heartbeat and respiration, the patient screamed, 'I am in hell!' He was terrified and pleaded with me to help him. I was scared to death. Then I noticed a genuinely alarmed look on his face. He had a look worse than the expression seen in death. His pupils were dilated and he was perspiring and trembling. He looked as if his hair was "on end." Dr. Rawlings is now a devoted Christian. He published a book called, "Beyond Death's Door" which describes the reality of hell that many people saw after their death on the operating table before they regained a heartbeat. Many of these people did not believe in God, the Bible, or hell prior to their near death experience.

There have been many descriptive studies of testimonials of people who died momentarily and regained a heartbeat. They recanted stories of being surrounded by grotesque human and animal forms, hearing other people moaning in pain and being tortured in a hell-like experience. Some of the researchers include British Researcher Margot Grey (1985), and sociologist Charles Flynn (1986). Jesus said in Mark 9:47, "And if thy eye offends thee pluck it out: it is better for thee to enter into the kingdom of God with one eye, than having two eyes to be cast into hell fire."

Scientists have determined the center of the earth is a burning hot fire that is hotter than the sun. In the Birmingham News, April 10, 1987, they had an article entitled, "The Earth's Center is Hotter than the Sun's Surface, Scientist's Say." The article stated that the scientists had recently discovered, "The Earth's inner core has a temperature of over 12,000 degrees Fahrenheit!" Jesus said in Luke 9:24. "For what is a man advantaged, if he shall gain the whole world, and lose himself, or be cast away?"

Thousands of years ago, the Bible described a place called hell as the prison of lost souls that rejected God, and as being located in the very heart of the earth deep below the earth's surface. And in the book of Revelation we see angels opening up a pit and smoke coming out of the earth with creatures during the great tribulation period.

The Location of Hell

Most people believe that Hell in located in the center of the earth. The Bible does describe hell as being somewhere beneath us. In the Bible in the Book of Acts, chapter 2, verse 31, the Bible says that after Jesus died, his soul went into hell. In Matthew 12:40 Jesus said, "For as Jonah was in the whale's belly: so shall He be three days and three nights in the heart of the earth." The Word of God reveals that hell is inside the earth. In Ephesians 4:9 the Bible teaches that Jesus went underneath the earth. Hell is underneath the earth (Isa. 14:9). In the last days, the angel of God will open up the pit: locusts will come out of it upon the earth to torture humanity (Rev. 9:2-3). And in verse 4: "And it was commanded them that they should not hurt the grass of the earth, neither any green thing, neither any tree; but only those men which have not the seal of God in their foreheads." There are surely demonic forces locked up underneath the earth.

Many people throughout time have published books, magazines, and have authored other works which indicate that hell is somewhere beneath us. Casper Peucer, a fourteenth century astronomer and physician, and Harold Sigurdsson, the author of, "Melting the Earth; The History of Ideas on Volcanic Eruptions," and many others have documented many cases of screams and cries coming out of volcanoes, and many have concluded that it had to be screams of tormented souls in the fires of hell below. The earth's crust is normally 40-50 miles thick and less than that if we are on the ocean floor. Researchers say that in part of the ocean's floor the earth's crust is less than a 1500 meters thick. Scientists have discovered cracks on the oceans floor where fire was leaking out. The book, "The Deep Sea" by Joseph Wallace (page 39) reads, "Perhaps the strangest creatures recently discovered are Riftia pachyptila, the giant tube worms. Measuring up to eight feet in length, the worms are only found near deep-sea vents. How does that correlate to the scriptures? Jesus said that hell is, "where their worm dieth not, and the fire is not quenched" (Mark 9:48).

Hell is a Place of Punishment and Fire

In Luke 16:24, Jesus spoke in a parable about a rich man that died and went to hell and the man said, "…I am tormented in this flame." He also requested some water and a preacher to go and warn his five brethren not to come to the place of punishment where he was. Obviously, he knew why he was in hell because he felt that if his brothers were warned they could stop what they were doing and not go to hell. The people that go to hell will remember their lives on the earth and what has brought them there.

In Matthew 13:42, Jesus said, "And shall cast them into a furnace of fire: there shall be wailing and gnashing of teeth."

In Matthew 25:41, Jesus will say to those on His left hand, "Depart from me, ye cursed, into everlasting fire prepared for the devil and his angels."

Revelation 20:15 states, "And whosoever was not found written in the Lamb's Book of Life was cast into the lake of fire."

Matthew 10:28: "Fear not them which kill the body, but are not able to kill the soul: but rather fear Him which is able to destroy both soul and body in hell."

Chapter Seven

The Final Judgments

The Time of Death is Unknown and All Will Go to Judgment

The Bible says in Hebrews 9:27, "…it is appointed to man once to die and after that the judgment," The Bible says that we brought nothing into this world and we will be carrying nothing out of it in our hands. Jesus said, "What shall it profit a man if he shall gain the whole world and lose his own soul? Or what shall a man give in exchange for his soul?" (Matt. 16:26) Wherever your soul is going you will not be taking anything with you. Now is the time to accept Jesus as your Lord and Savior, before it is too late. Death is like a car accident. The time of it is uncertain and it can have an element of surprise and the time of our departure can be an unpredictable event. The location of it cannot always be predicted. And just how bad it will be won't be known until you go through it. Young people go to the hospital and find out that they have only two weeks to live. Cancer or some other disease has come to take them. Will your soul be lost forever, or will you repent and turn away from your sins, turn to Jesus, and surrender your life to Him in exchange for eternal life? The Bible says in Ecclesiastes 8:8, "There is no man that hath power over his spirit to retain the spirit; neither hath he power in the day of death: and there is no discharge in that war: neither shall wickedness deliver those that are given to it." And Jesus said in John 10:27-28, "My sheep hear my voice, and I know them and they follow me: And I give unto them eternal life; and they shall never perish, neither shall any man pluck them out of my Father's hand. Do you have eternal life?"

Skeletons and Our Secrets Will Come Out of Their Closets

The scripture says, "For God shall bring every work into judgment, with every secret thing, whether it be good, or whether it be evil" (Eccl. 12:14). You will one day stand before an Almighty God who has the power to either save or destroy both your body and your soul forever. All hidden and secret things will be revealed before the entire universe. The Bible says, be sure of this one thing, "… be sure your sin will find you out," in Numbers 32:23. God knows about our sins. The Bible tells us, "The eyes of the Lord are going to and fro beholding the good and the evil." Keep in mind that Jesus told His own disciples, "For there is nothing covered that shall not be revealed nor hid that shall not be made known and come abroad" (Matt. 10:26).

The Great White Throne Judgment

The Bible reveals in Revelation that God is sitting on a Great White Throne and the dead shall stand before him (Revelation 20:11-15). The books are going to be opened and the Book of Life and the dead who are now in front of God are judged out of those things written in the books according to their works. The Bible says that whoever was not found written in the Lamb's Book of Life was cast into the Lake of Fire. The dead will answer to God Almighty about their works whether they were good or evil. Some think that Christians will not be at this judgment, but Jesus said that the hour is coming when they that "are in the graves shall hear His voice and shall come forth; they that have done good unto the resurrection of life, and they that have done evil, unto the resurrection of damnation" (John 5:28-29). Many who profess Christianity will in fact be at the Great White Throne judgment and go into the Lake of Fire based on Jesus' own words. Jesus said that many would say unto him in that day, Lord, Lord, have we not prophesied, cast out devils, and done many wonderful works and he declared that he would profess unto them to depart from him as they were workers of iniquity (Matthew 7:21-24).

In the gospel of Matthew, chapter 25 verses 31-46, it says that Jesus will come with his angels and gather all nations together and shall separate the sheep in his right hand from the goats in his left hand. The goats will go into everlasting fire. They are the ones who did not visit the sick, help the needy or homeless, go to the prisons, or clothe the naked.

What Will Happen on Judgment Day?

The Bible says, "For we all must appear before the judgment seat of Christ; that every one may receive the things done in his body, according to that he hath done, whether it be good or bad" (II Corinthians 5:10). The Bible says, "…every one of us shall give an account of himself to God" (Romans:14:12). So you will stand before God to answer him about your life story and everything you've done or have failed to do. Jesus said that "…every idle word that men shall speak, they shall give an account thereof on the Day of Judgment," (Matthew 12:36). According to the Book of Ecclesiastes 12:14, "…God will bring every work into judgment, with every secret thing, whether it be good or evil." There has been no sin that has been hidden that God will not bring to the light. Salvation is a free gift that Jesus gives to those that accept Him, repent, and believe. People say, "I am saved" and it's all right to believe that you are saved. Remember that Jesus said it is he that endures until the end that shall be saved (Matthew 24:13). I studied at great length the doctrines of eternal security and predestination. God will let us know on Judgment Day whether we are saved, and whether or not He's given us grace and our sins are forgiven, or whether to depart from Him to the Lake of Fire with the Devil and his angels because of our deplorable, despicable, wicked sins which were not repented of. God has a choice. Many have been deceived and will not enter into heaven (Matthew 7:21-24). The question becomes as to whether or not they were converted and saved in the first place. Shall men continue in sin that grace may abound? God forbid (Rom. 6:1). It would be proud, boastful, and presumptions to make ourselves the judge and to declare that we will undoubtedly be in heaven unless you know for sure you are saved. God is the judge. Search your ways and your heart and be sure that you belong to Jesus. Our Bible says, "Nevertheless, the foundation of God standeth sure, having this seal, The Lord knoweth those that are his, and let every one that nameth the name of Christ depart from iniquity (2 Tim. 2:19-20). Jesus said,"Not every one that saith unto me Lord, Lord, shall enter into the kingdom of heaven: but he that doeth the will of my Father which is in heaven. Many will say to me in that day, Lord, Lord, have we not prophesied in thy name? And in thy name cast out devils? And in thy name done many wonderful works? And then I will profess to them, I never knew you: depart from me ye that work iniquity" (Matthew 7:21-23).

The Bible says, "There is one lawgiver, who is able to save and to destroy: who art thou that judgest another?" (James 4:12) The free gift of grace is God's sovereign choice and He will examine our works and inform us whether or not he has granted us grace and everlasting life or everlasting damnation. Notice carefully what is recorded about keeping God's commandments in the Revelation. The Bible declares,"Blessed are they that do his commandments that they may have the right to the tree of life, and may enter in through the gates into the city. For without (are) dogs, and sorcerers, and whoremongers, and murderers, and idolaters, and whosoever loveth and maketh a lie. I Jesus have sent mine angel to testify unto you these things in the churches. I am the root and the offspring of David, and the bright and morning star" (Rev. 22:14-16). Jesus makes it clear that he sent his messenger into the churches to testify these things. A true church will testify to the people the things which Jesus said. The people must get the message as to what God is looking for and what he is expecting out of them. All ways do not lead to heaven. God forbids that we continue to sin that grace may abound once we are forgiven (Romans 6:1). Jesus wants and to repent and not to turn back again and again.

Is it Possible to Think You Are a Christian and Belong to Satan?

Dear Brother or Sister, when you confess that Jesus is Lord, and believe that He died for your sins, and you repent of those sins by turning away from them, then accept him as your Lord and personal Savior and have become born again and spirit filled. The Holy Ghost guides you into truth and righteousness. You are a work in progress and you are saved from hell. When you've done that sincerely from your heart and have been renewed by the Holy Spirit God will strengthen you to live a godly lifestyle. When you sin you are surrendering yourself back to Satan's control, and you are in danger of eternal damnation if you don't come back to Jesus and stay away from Satan. The Bible warns that in the last days that men will depart from the faith. The Bible says, "He that committeth sin is of the Devil, for the Devil sinneth from the beginning. For this purpose the Son of God was manifested, that He might destroy the works of the Devil" (I John 3:8). Don't be tricked.

Sin is Satan's work. Don't let the Devil deceive you into a life-long habit of sinning. God can forgive you if you do sin. First John 1:9 says, "If we confess our sins, He is faithful and just to forgive us our sins, and cleanse us from all unrighteousness." Sin is Satan's deception and when you sin you officially make an agreement with the Devil. And that is why the entire human race was ruined in the Garden of Eden. Now is the time to repent of sins such as lying, backbiting, stealing, adultery, fornication, (which is premarital sex), profanity, wrath, unforgiveness, blasphemy, witchcraft, adultery, homosexuality, lesbianism, and rebellion, which is disobedience to parents or authorities. Jesus is waiting for us to confess and repent and come back to him. He doesn't want to use us and then have to let Satan use us because of our rebellion. Jesus said, "No man can serve two masters..." (Matt. 6:24). Jesus compared the Kingdom of Heaven to a net that caught good fish and bad, and brought both to the shore, and then the fishermen kept the good fish and threw away the bad. He said that the angels will separate the wicked from the just and put the wicked into a furnace of fire and there shall be wailing and gnashing of teeth (Matt. 13:47-50). Jesus said, "... the children of the kingdom shall be cast into outer darkness..." (Matt. 8:12).

"Ye are of your father, the devil, and the lusts of your father ye will do" (John 8:44). Watch your passions! Many yield to Satan and still do religious activities and attend church, and because of that they feel they belong to God, but they're being fooled. Jesus said that not everyone that says Lord, Lord, shall enter into the Kingdom of Heaven, but he that doeth the will of My Father in heaven.

The Bible says, "Whosoever is born of God does not commit sin, for his seed remains in him; and he cannot sin, because he is born of God. In this the children of God are manifest, and the children of the devil: whosoever doeth not righteousness is not of God, neither he that loveth not his brother" (I John 3:9-10).

Simply believing in Jesus is not enough, for the Bible says that faith without works (actions) is dead. Even the devils believe there is one God and tremble (James 2:19). One can believe and be a practicing witch or harlot. Saving faith is always followed by good fruit, which is the evidence that we now belong to Christ and have broken up with The Devil. Jesus said that we cannot serve two masters (Matthew 6:24).

The good news is that sin was judged on the cross of Christ and Jesus was nailed on that cross so that we would not have to go to the Lake of Fire at His Great White Throne Judgment. Repent now and believe the gospel before time runs out! Ask Jesus to fill you with the gift and power of the Holy Ghost as he did when the church began.

The Heart is Set to do Evil When Judgment is Delayed

The Bible says, "Because sentence against an evil work is not executed speedily, therefore the heart of the sons of men is fully set in them to do evil" (Eccl. 8:11). Many people do not stop doing things that they know is wrong if they don't believe that immediate consequences will occur. Jesus said in Luke 13:3, "Except you repent, you shall likewise perish." Keep in mind that Jesus said this to compare the end of the sinners who won't repent to the fate of the Galileans who were murdered as a human sacrifice and to compare the destiny of an unrepentant sinner to the eighteen people who the tower of Siloam fell on and killed. Jesus was plainly warning the sinners who lacked a repentant heart of his or her destiny and ultimate end because of his sin which includes "the second death" which is the lake of fire and brimstone described in the final book (Revelation 21:8).

Examples of Divine Judgment in the Bible

God destroyed the earth with a flood during the days of Noah and saved only Noah and his family. Why? They obeyed God, built and got into the Ark as He said (2 Pet. 2:5). Jesus warned us that at the time of his return to earth that people would be just like they were during the days of Noah, eating, drinking, and getting married all the way up until the flood came. Don't wait until the door is closed and the time is up. The day and hour of his return is not known but it is soon. Noah's Ark is still on Mount Ararat today! The Turkey government has built a museum about the Ark. Jesus said, "I am the way, the truth, and the life" (John 14:6). The Ark was the only way to be saved then and Jesus is the only way to be saved now!

Archaeologists have discovered the ruins of the cities that were destroyed by fire and brimstone that fell from the sky during biblical days. They have confirmed that the brimstone fell from the sky and that the fire started on the rooftops. God destroyed the cities of Sodom and Gomorrah by raining fire from the sky and saved only Lot and his family. Lot's wife looked back and turned into a pillar of salt. The cities have been left as an example for those that would live ungodly (Peter 2:6). In other words, make your decision that you are coming out (of the world) and don't look back on your way out.

Jesus said to His disciples, "Remember Lot's wife", in Luke 17:32. That was a warning. She was turned to a pillar of salt because of disobedience and looking back. It is important that each one of us is reminded that God does not want us to look back into our old sinful ways once we are forgiven. The word of God reminds us that if any man be in Christ he is a new creature and those old things have passed away. God did not let Moses enter the Promised Land because of sin. This was an act of judgment by God.

God saved all of the people out of the land of Egypt and destroyed all of them in the wilderness except Joshua and Caleb because of unbelief, sin, murmuring and complaining. The adults could not enter the Promised Land, but their children were allowed to see it (Jude 5).

God kicked Lucifer (now known as Satan) and his angels out of heaven because of sin. "How art thou fallen from heaven, O Lucifer, son of the morning? How art thou cut down to the ground, which didst weaken the nations! For thou hast said in thine heart, I will ascend into heaven, I will exalt my throne above the stars of God: I will sit also upon the mount of the congregation, in the sides of the north: I will ascend above the heights of the clouds; I will be like the most High. Yet thou shalt be brought down to hell, to the sides of the pit" (Isa. 14:12). God can also blot a person's name out of the Lamb's Book of Life, which is where your name needs to be or you will not be invited to spend eternity in heaven.

Jesus Will Separate the Wheat from the Tares

The Devil has planted his own tares in the visible church among the wheat. The tares are called the children of the devil and they resemble the wheat but belong to Satan. "Another parable put he forth unto them, saying, the kingdom of heaven is likened unto a man which sowed good seed in his field: But while men slept, his enemy came and sowed tares among the wheat, and went his way. But when the blade was sprung up, and brought forth fruit, then appeared the tares also. So the servants of the householder came and said unto him, Sir, didst not thou sow good seed in thy field? from whence then hath it tares? He said unto them, An enemy hath done this."

Matthew 13:30 says, "Let both grow together until the harvest: and in the time of harvest I will say to the reapers, Gather ye together first the tares, and bind them in bundles to burn them: but gather the wheat into my barn."

Matthew 13:41-42 explains, "The Son of man shall send forth his angels, and they shall gather out of his kingdom all things that offend, and them which do iniquity; and shall cast them into a furnace of fire: there shall be wailing and gnashing of teeth."

The Bible says, "And he shall set the sheep on his right hand, but the goats on the left" (Matthew 25:33). And in Matthew 25:41 He warns, "Then shall he say also unto them on the left hand, Depart from me, ye cursed, into everlasting fire, prepared for the devil and his angels." Do not allow Satan's servants, false ministers, or deceived people to trick you out of your soul. It is all a disguise costume in some cases and Jesus warned that the thief comes but to kill, steal, and to destroy. Don't be fooled by serpents in pulpits that are out to get your money but have forgotten your soul. Beware of wolves that come to you in the sheep's clothing. Are they preaching the same thing as Jesus, Peter, Paul, James, and John? Jesus sent them out and told them that both repentance and remission of sins would be preached in his name among all nations beginning at Jerusalem! What are they teaching and preaching?

ALL Men Will Stand Before the Almighty God

The Bible says, "So then every one of us shall give account of himself to God"

(Romans 14:12). All men shall stand before God and all skeletons will come out of the closet.

The Bible declares, "For if we would judge ourselves, we should not be judged. But when we are judged, we are chastened of the Lord, that we should not be condemned with the world" (I Corinthians 11:31-32).

God will chastise (punish, rebuke, discipline) us now to correct us so that he won't have to send us into the Lake of Fire later.

We should look at some tribulation as God's loving hand to refine and shape our character into the type of person that God desires to shape us into. The goldsmith uses fire to purge and refine gold.

Jesus said, "But I say unto you, that every idle word that men shall speak, they shall give account thereof in the Day of Judgment. For by thy words thou shalt be justified, and by thy words thou shalt be condemned" (Matthew 12:36-37).

I am aware that some of our Bible scholars would like to say that Jesus' words were to a Jewish audience under the law and that it did not apply to us in the dispensation of Grace. I want to remind the reader that the words of Jesus was both to the Jewish audience and to each generation to come. One has to just briefly glimpse at the warnings to the church of Thyatira in the book of Revelation. Jesus declared that he gave Jezebel time to repent of her fornication and adultery and she did not. Jesus then declared in his own words to the church that he was going to kill Jezebel and her children with death because she refused to repent. He said he would throw her into a bed and them which did adultery with her into tribulation. He then says he is the one that searches the depths of the heart and gives to everyone according to their deeds. We should see from Jesus' own warnings that his words to repent or perish in the gospels and other declarations in the gospels also applies to us in the dispensation and covenant of grace. Repent or Perish.

We must be careful what we say when we are upset. We must repent when or if we say things to hurt or damage others. Words can send you to hell on Judgment Day, which can include what we say about others. Repent of the things that you may have said to curse others. The tongue is an unruly evil full of deadly poison (James 3:8). Blessings and cursings should not proceed out of the same mouth (James 3:10). Can a fountain bring both sweet water and bitter water forward out of the same fountain (James 3:11)?

What about Anger and Name Calling?

The Bible says, "Ye have heard that it was said of them of old time, Thou shalt not kill; and whosoever shall kill shall be in danger of the judgment: But I say unto you, That whosoever is angry with his brother without a cause shall be in danger of the judgment: and whosoever shall say to his brother, Raca, (meaning, empty one, fool, empty head; and is expressive of great contempt) shall be in danger of the council: but whosoever shall say, Thou fool, shall be in danger of hell fire" (Matt. 5:21-22). We must apologize to others and ask for their forgiveness. Words can damage an individual mind and emotions so bad that it can wreck and ruin their lives due to their emotional health. We can murder people with words which is why we must repent of every evil or idle word which we have spoken to others in haste or deliberately with malice.

Pluck it out!

Jesus said, "And if thy right eye offends thee, pluck it out, and cast it from thee: for it is profitable for thee that one of thy members should perish, and not that thy whole body should be cast into hell" (Matthew 5:29). Hell is real and we should not take anything that Jesus said lightly. The Holy Spirit comes to gives us power to walk in the spirit and to overcome the works of the flesh.

Pluck it out. Jesus said, "For whoever will save his life shall lose it; but whoever will lose his life for my sake, the same shall save it" (Luke 9:25). What is it today that you are hanging on to that can keep you out of heaven? Jesus said to pluck it out. Yes it will hurt you to get rid of some of the old luggage in the trunk or some things down in the basement but it will hurt you more later if you keep it. It is evident that what we do with our body parts could cause us to be cast into hell. Is it really worth it in the end? Take some time to think about that one night stand or any secret rendezvous that you have not altogether quit or may not have sincerely repented of. Consider the friends who cause you to stumble and fall or how you fall to temptation if you go to the liquor store. What happens when you see the dope dealer or the man that you ended the affair with? Are you allowing women to seduce you out of your very soul? Think about the secret lovers who cause you to stumble and fall into the devil's trap. What shall any pleasure profit us in the end if we lose our soul and become eternally damned? It is not wise for any recovering addict to go to any location where he or she can find someone to support the old habits. Straight is the gate and narrow is the way and few there be that find it! (Matthew 7:13-14) Jesus said, "No man having put his hand to the plow, and looking back, is fit (ready) for the kingdom of God" (Luke 9:62). Secrets will be brought to the light and discussed openly before everybody. The Bible says "For God shall bring every work into judgment, with every secret thing, whether it be good, or whether it be evil" (Ecclesiastes 12:14).

Secrets Will Be Brought to the Light.
Persevere Until the End.

The Bible declares, "Some men's sins are open beforehand, going before to judgment; and some men they follow after. Likewise also, the good works of some are manifest beforehand; and they that are otherwise cannot be hid" (I Timothy 5:24-25). It shall be known and come abroad during this life or this next one as to precisely what our works are.

Open sin will be discussed at the judgment and sins that are hidden will be brought into the light. The Bible says, "There is nothing covered that shall not be revealed and hid that shall not be made known" (Matt.10:26). Some sins will be exposed in this life before the judgment and anything that is not known abroad will surely be brought to the light in the final judgment. The Bible says in First Peter 4:18, "And if the righteous shall scarcely be saved, where shall the ungodly and the sinner appear?" "The time is come that judgment must begin at the house of God (churches): and if it first begin at us, what shall the end be of them that obey not the gospel of God" (1 Peter 4:17)? The word scarcely here means, "That few of the professing righteous shall persevere until the very end and be saved". Jesus warned the church of Laodicea by saying, "I know thy works, that thou art neither cold nor hot. So then because thou art lukewarm, and neither cold nor hot, I will spue (vomit) thee out of my mouth" (Rev. 3:15-16).

Each Church Shall be Judged

The Bible says, "For the time is come that judgment must begin at the house of God: and if it first begin at us, what shall the end be of them that obey not the gospel of God? And if the righteous scarcely be saved, where shall the ungodly and the sinner appear? Wherefore let them that suffer according to the will of God commit the keeping of their souls to him in well doing, as unto a faithful Creator" (I Peter 4:17-18).

How Do You Know if People Are Truly What They Say They Are?

The Bible says, "They profess that they know God; but in works they deny him, being abominable, and disobedient, and unto every good work reprobate" (Titus 1:16). Jesus told us in Matthew 7:16 that you would know them by their fruits. Do men gather grapes of thorns or figs of thistles, he asked. He then explained, "Every tree that brings not forth good fruit is hewn down, and cast into the fire" (Matthew 7:19). The scriptures testify, "Whosoever is born of God doth not commit sin; for his seed remaineth in him: and he cannot sin, because he is born of God. In this the children of God are manifest, and the children of the devil: whosoever doeth not righteousness is not of God, neither he that loveth not his brother" (1 John 3:9-10). The fact is that once you are a Christian you belong to Jesus. A Christian cannot practice sin as a lifestyle habit and do the exact things which the world does. He or she is a new creature and is born again. For example, there is no such a thing as a Christian who is also a pimp or a practicing witch.

Don't Fall for the Devil's Game

The Bible says, "Be sober, be vigilant; because your adversary the devil, as a roaring lion, walks about, seeking whom he may devour." (I Peter 5:8). Satan wants to destroy you. He is called the God of this world in Second Corinthians 4:4 and is said to blind the minds of those who don't believe in the same verse. No wonder 1 John 2:15 says, "Love not the world neither the things that are in the world. If any man loves the world, the love of the Father is not in him. For all that is in the world, the lust of the flesh, and the lust of the eyes, and the pride of life, is not of the Father, (God) but is of the world. Satan uses every demonic trick and this world as his platform and stage to seduce the souls of humankind. He advertises all that is against the Word of God and God himself and glorifies sin in television, movies, magazines, books, music, entertainment, politics, and the worldly systems. He uses lies, half-truths, seduction, flattery, sorcery, witchcraft, drugs, food including fast foods and unhealthy foods, worldly entertainment, music, television, internet, pornography, idols, magic, false teachers, sex, money, worldly ambitions, lust for power, money, and sex, and especially false teachers and religion. He works in the pride of man and uses the media, movies, television, books, magazines, and people to lure mankind into his game of deception, sin, devil worship and destruction. Movies, television, books, and most things you can see are part of the setup to seduce man into idols, devil worship, fornication,

adultery, murder, revenge, and all that is against God. The goal
of The Devil is to destroy every soul and to ruin each adult and
child permanently and to have them thrown into the lake of fire
that burns with fire and brimstone in Revelation 21:8.

Announce to Everyone Publicly That You Belong to Jesus!

Jesus declared, "Whosoever therefore shall confess me before
men, him will I confess also before my Father which is in heaven.
But whosoever shall deny me before men, him will I also deny
before my Father which is in heaven" (Matthew 10:32-33). The
people who are believers in Jesus must be true to who they are
and what they are to each unbeliever and skeptic regardless of
the persecution, criticism, rejection, betrayal, and hatred that re-
sults. Think about it for a moment, many sinners who profess no
faith in God are not ashamed to say what they are including the
most ungodly and profane. Jesus said, "You are the light of the
world. A city that is set on a hill cannot be hid" (Matthew 5:14).

Don't Be a Hypocrite and Say One Thing but Do Another!

How do we know people are saved? The Bible says, "He that saith,
I know him, and keepeth not his commandments, is a liar, and the
truth is not in him." (I John 2:4). Don't just hear God's Word, but
obey the truth and lifestyle it teaches. A hypocrite is a pretender
and the word literally means to hide behind a mask. Jesus called
the Pharisees hypocrites in Matthew 23:28 and said, "Even so you
outwardly appear righteous unto men but within you are full of
hypocrisy and iniquity." Woe unto you, scribes and Pharisees,
hypocrites! For you are like the white graves (sepulchers), which
indeed appear beautiful outward, but are within full of dead men's
bones and of all uncleanness (Matt. 23:27). Everyone who profess-
es to know The Lord Jesus doesn't know the Lord Jesus. Jesus said,
"Beware of false prophets, which come to you in sheep's clothing,

but inwardly they are ravening wolves" in Matthew 7:15. Jesus also warned us the thirteenth chapter of the book of Matthew that the enemy (Satan) would plant tares (his own children) in the church with the wheat (children of God) and that angels would separate them by throwing them (tares-children of the devil) into the furnace of fire at the end of the world (Matt. 13:24-42).

Be a Doer of the Word

James said, "But be ye doers of the word, and not hearers only, deceiving your own selves. For if any be a hearer of the word, and not a doer, he is like unto a man beholding his natural face in a glass: For he beholdeth himself, and goeth his way, and straightway forgetteth what manner of man he was" (James 1:22-24). The first married couple, Adam and Eve heard the Word of God but did not do what God said. The sin caused the ruin of the entire human race and their children were also affected and you and I. The Bible says "For it had been better for them not to have known the way of righteousness, than, after they have known it, to turn from the holy commandment delivered unto them" (II Peter 2:22).

If You Die Today Are You Prepared to Meet God?

The Word of God testifies, "And as it is appointed unto men once to die, but after this the judgment" (Hebrews 9:27). Don't be fooled. The sinners are not saved and the ungodly are lost, even if they profess to be saved. The scriptures also teach us, "Little children, let no man deceive you: he that doeth righteousness is righteous, even as he is righteous. He that committeth sin is of the devil; for the devil sinneth from the beginning. For this purpose the Son of God was manifested, that he might destroy the works of the devil" (I John 3:7-8). It can be hard to digest for many of us that sincere Bible believing Christians are not yet converted or saved. Nevertheless, we must take God at his word.

What to Do With Friends Who Are a Bad Influence

The Bible says, "Be not deceived: evil communications corrupt good manners" (I Corinthians 15:33). Bad company corrupts good morals. The scriptures also teach, "Be ye not unequally yoked together with unbelievers: for what fellowship hath righteousness with unrighteousness? and what concord hath light with darkness" (I Corinthians 6:14).

Come out from among them and be ye separate, saith the Lord, and touch not the unclean thing, and I will receive you. If you know that someone causes you to struggle with sin or that they are a bad influence, separate yourself (I Corinthians 6:17).

God Warns Us Before Destruction!

The time has arrived where people don't want to hear God's truth as prophesied and foretold in the Bible!

"For the time will come that they will not endure sound doctrine; but after their own LUSTS shall heap to themselves teachers, having itching ears; And shall turn away their ears from the TRUTH, and shall be turned into fables" (2 Tim. 4:3-4).

People will no longer listen to the truth but only to what they what to hear.

People in many churches believe lies and have delusions because they enjoy unrighteousness.

"Even him, whose coming is after the working of Satan with all power and signs and LYING WONDERS. And with all deceivableness of unrighteousness in them that perish; because they received not the love of the truth that they might be saved. AND for this cause GOD SHALL SEND THEM STRONG DELUSION, that they should believe a lie. That they all might be DAMNED who believed not the truth, BUT HAD PLEASURE in UNRIGHTEOUSNESS" (2 Thess. 2:9-11).

The desires of folks are turning them against Christ and

they are in danger of damnation.

"...But the younger widows refuse: FOR they have begun to WAX WANTON AGAINST CHRIST, they will marry, having DAMNATION, because they have CAST OFF THEIR FIRST FAITH" (1 Tim. 5:11-12).

Men have snuck into the churches and on television that are not even Christians nor born again and have been totally undetected. They are denying the very Lord they talk about.

"For CERTAIN MEN HAVE CREPT IN UNAWARES, who were before of old ordained to this condemnation, ungodly men, turning the grace of our God into lasciviousness (the state or habitual condition of feeling an excessive or morbid sexual desire), and denying the only Lord God, and our Lord Jesus Christ" (Jude 4).

People are turning back into the lifestyles that they had prior to coming to know the Lord!

"For it had been better for them not to have known the way of righteousness, than, after they have known it, to turn from the holy commandment delivered unto them. But it happened according to the true proverb, the dog is turned to his vomit again; and the sow that was washed to her wallowing in the mire" (2 Peter 2:21-22).

God reminded us of how he destroyed the Hebrews who were once saved.

"I will therefore put to your remembrance, though you once knew this, how that the Lord, having saved the people out of the land of Egypt, afterward destroyed them that believed not. And the angels, who kept not their first estate, but left their own habitation, he hath reserved in everlasting chains under darkness unto the judgment of the great day. Even as Sodom and Gomorrah, and the cities about them in like manner, giving themselves over to fornication, and going after strange flesh, are set forth for an example, suffering the vengeance of eternal fire" (Jude 5-7).

Some who fall into the Devil's trap of sin will not be able to repent again.

"For it is impossible for those who were once enlightened, and have tasted of the heavenly gift, and were made partakers of the Holy Ghost, And have tasted of the good word of God, and the powers of the world to come, If they fall away, to renew them again unto repentance; seeing they crucify to themselves the Son of God afresh, and put him to an open shame" (Heb. 6:4-6).

Whoever willfully and deliberately practices sin is considered God's adversary.

"For if we sin willfully after that we have received the knowledge of the truth, there remains no more sacrifice for sins, but a certain fearful looking for of judgment and fiery indignation, which shall devour the adversaries. He that despised Moses' law died without mercy under two or three witnesses: Of how much sorer punishment, suppose ye, shall he be thought worthy, who hath trodden under foot the Son of God, and hath counted the blood of the covenant, wherewith he was sanctified, an unholy thing, and hath done despite the spirit of Grace?" (Heb. 10:27-29)

It is a terrifying experience to be in God's very hands if He is upset with us!

"It is a fearful thing to fall into the hands of the living God" (Heb. 10:31).

Some will depart from the faith and be seduced by lies and doctrines of demons!

"Now the spirit speaketh expressly, that in the latter times some shall depart from the faith, giving heed to seducing spirits and doctrines of devils; Speaking lies in hypocrisy; having their conscience seared with a hot iron" (1 Tim. 4:1-2).

Some of the very angels of God were cast down to hell and the whole planet was destroyed in a flood. Cities were also destroyed by fire, which fell from the sky. We must take heed that

we are not destroyed in the end and we have been duly warned.

"For if God spared not the angels that sinned, but cast them down to hell, and delivered them into chains of darkness, to be reserved unto judgment; And spared not the old world, but saved Noah the eighth person, a preacher of righteousness, bringing in the flood upon the world of the ungodly; And turning the cities of Sodom and Gomorrah to ashes condemned them with an overthrow, making them an example unto those that after should live ungodly; And delivered just Lot, vexed with the filthy conversation of the wicked: (For that righteous man dwelling among them, in seeing and hearing, vexed his righteous soul from day to day with their unlawful deeds)" (2 Pet. 2:4-8).

God knows how to bring people out of temptation if they want to come out.

"The Lord knoweth how to deliver the godly out of temptation and to reserve the unjust unto the Day of Judgment to be PUNISHED" (2 Pet. 2:9)."But these, as natural brute beasts, made to be taken and destroyed, speak evil of the things that they understand not; and shall utterly perish in their own corruption; and shall receive the reward of unrighteousness, as THEY COUNT IT PLEASURE TO RIOT IN THE DAY TIME. Spots they are and blemishes, sporting themselves with their own deceiving while they feast with you: Having EYES full OF ADULTERY, and that cannot cease from sin; BEGUILING UNSTABLE SOULS: an heart they have exercised with covetous practices; cursed children: Which have forsaken the right way, and are gone astray, following the way of Balaam the son of Bosor, who loved the wages of unrighteousness: But was rebuked for his iniquity: the dumb ass speaking with man's voice forbad the madness of the prophet" (2 Pet. 2:12-16).

The scriptures teach, "Having a form of godliness but denying the power thereof; from such turn away. For of this sort are they which creep into houses, and lead captive silly women laden with sins, led away with diverse lusts, Ever learning AND NEVER ABLE TO COME TO THE KNOWLEDGE OF THE TRUTH" (2 Tim. 3:5-6). "Now as Jannes and Jambres withstood Moses, so do these also RESIST THE TRUTH: men of corrupt minds, reprobate concerning THE FAITH. But they shall proceed no further: for their folly shall be manifest unto all men, as theirs also was" (2 Tim. 3:8-9).

"Wherefore he saith, Awake thou that sleepest, and arise from the dead, and Christ shall give thee light. See then that ye walk circumspectly, not as fools, but as wise, redeeming the time for the days are evil" (Eph. 5:14-16). "Thou believest there is One God: thou doest well: the devils also believe, and tremble. But wilt thou know, O vain man, that faith without works is dead?" (James 2:19-20). "Nevertheless the foundation of God standeth sure, having this seal; The Lord knoweth them that are his. And let every one that nameth the name of Christ depart from iniquity" (2 Tim. 2:19). "For the time is come that judgment must begin at the house of God: and if it begin at us, what shall the end be of them that obey not the gospel of God? And if the righteous shall scarcely be saved, where shall the ungodly and the sinner appear?" (1 Pet. 4:17-18).

How Does One Know if They Are Not Truly a Follower of Jesus?

The Bible says, "Be sober and vigilant because your adversary the Devil walks about as a roaring lion, seeking whom he may devour" (I Peter 5:8). According to Revelation 20:3, the Devil will be thrown into the bottomless pit so he can't deceive the nations any longer. Satan is a deceiver. Don't let him fool you.

First John 3:8 says, "He that committeth sin is of the Devil; for the Devil sinneth from the beginning. For this purpose was the Son of God manifested, that he might destroy the works of the Devil."

According to Ephesians 2:2, Satan is the prince of the power of the air; the spirit that is working in the children of disobedience. If you disobey God, it is Satan that is working in you and you belong to him. You either belong to God or to Satan. (There is no third choice.) If you want to belong to God you must admit you are a sinner, accept Jesus, repent of your sins, turn away from them, and believe that Jesus has given you his gift of eternal life because of the death, burial and resurrection of Him from the dead for your sins and then live according to God's holy commandments. The excuses that you make up for your sins are coming from Satan. He told Adam and Eve a lie in the Garden of Eden and said that God is aware that you will become as God if you eat the forbidden fruit of the tree. He gave them an excuse to sin against God.

Chapter Eight

Who is in Danger of Going to Hell and The Good News

Hell is for those that reject Jesus and his sacrifice for their sins on the cross. Hell is for those that refuse to acknowledge to God that they are a sinner, and ask him for grace. Hell is for those that refuse to believe that Jesus is the Son of God and that His sacrifice on the cross is the only ransom for their sins. Hell is for those that refuse to repent of their sins by forsaking the actual practice of sins, which exclude one from heaven. Hell is for those that continue to serve Satan, and to disobey God willfully with no true intent to do anything else. The Bible tells us in Revelation 21:8 that certain types of sin will bring people to hell.

Liars, Whoremongers, the Abominable, Murderers, Sorcerers, Unbelievers, Homosexuals, Lesbians, Witches, etc.

In Revelation 21:8, the Bible says, and I quote, "But the fearful, and unbelieving (those cowardly and those who don't believe that Jesus is the Son of God and that He can save them from their sins)...and the abominable..." The Bible calls many things an abomination in the scripture including, "men with men and

women with women." "For this reason God gave them up to vile
passions. For even their women exchanged the natural use for
what is against nature. Likewise also, the men, leaving the natural
use of the woman, burned in their lust for one another, men with
men committing what is shameful, and receiving in themselves
the penalty of their error which was due" (Rom. 1:26-27). The
Bible says that if a man lies and has sex with a man as if he were
a woman, he has committed an abomination (Lev. 18:22; 20:13).
He then mentions murderers. Did you know that you don't have
to kill somebody to be a murderer? The Bible says that "Whosoever hates his brother is a murderer, and no murderer has eternal
life in Him" (1 John 3:15). Repent of all hatred especially hatred
for those who are in the church. He then says the whoremongers
who are those that habitually patronize prostitutes. The whoremonger would also be the lady who gets paid by men to provide
for men any form of sexual pleasure. The word whoremonger
comes from the Greek word pornea which is sometimes translated to English as whoremonger and sometimes as fornicator.
The whoremonger is anyone (male or female) who has sexual
contact outside of the marital relationship. A married person or
a single person can be a whoremonger if they have sexual relationships outside of marriage. The adulterer is a specific type of
a whoremonger. Adulterers are those that have a sexually loose
lifestyle outside of marriage. He then mentions that sorcerers
shall not enter heaven but the Lake of fire also. The word sorcery
comes from the original Greek word which means to use of mind
altering drugs. Sorcery includes but is not limited to using or
distributing illegal drugs. The use of the drugs was common in
the practice of witchcraft to activate the pineal gland to allow demons to gain access to the brain. The pineal gland is considered
to be the third eye and the window to the soul. Idolaters are those
that love money, sex, careers, amusements, food, music, world-

ly things and other things more than God. He finally says that all liars shall have their part in the lake, which burns with fire and brimstone, which is the second death. Lie detectors catch liars because the heart rate changes when one lies. Lies can cause health issues and heart problems. The Bible teaches us that The Devil is a liar and the father of lies (John 8:44). Repent of all lies. Lies are the works of Satan. He was a murderer from the beginning and abode not in the truth, because there is no truth in him (John 8:44). God loves the unbelievers (atheists) and homosexuals and all liars. Nevertheless, all sinners must repent or perish. The abominable shall have their part in the lake of fire that burns with brimstone.

We know that whosoever is born of God sins not; but he that is begotten of God keeps himself, and that wicked one touches him not (1 John 5:18). Repent of all of these sins and turn from them. Jesus said except you repent you shall likewise perish (Luke 13:5). You know for sure that you have repented if you have quit the sin.

Fornicators

The center for Disease and control in Atlanta, Georgia have informed the general public that condoms as they are made and designed do have microscopic holes in them and that although they do prevent pregnancy they cannot stop the spread of the HIV virus. The microscopic holes in condoms are small enough for a strand of the HIV virus to infect others. That alone should cause everyone to rethink their position on whether or not that fornication with condoms is safe and whether or not they ought to obey the Word of God. He goes to her like the ox that goes to the slaughter and as a fool to the correction of stocks. Till a dart strikes his liver, as a bird caught in a snare, and know not it is for his life (Prov. 7:22-23).

Researchers from the Medical Institute for Sexual Health in Austin studied the brain chemicals involved with the brain and the emotions as it relates to sex. Sex secretes an almost unbreakable bond forever with the sex partner. The act of sex before marriage and outside of marriage causes the brain, according to research, to have problems bonding emotionally and physically to one person (other than whoever one has become intimate with) because of the brains chemical attachment, addiction, and bonding with another partner or various partners. Settling down with or staying with one person is difficult due to fornication (sex before or outside of marriage).

The chemical Oxytocin is released in the brain of females and causes the lady to bond to a man psychologically and physically. Vasopressin is the male chemical that causes him to bond physically and psychologically with the female. The chemicals involved in the brain, memory, bonding, and emotional involvement causes problems settling down with one person if the person has had more than one sex partner. Sex is like tape that loses its ability to stick to objects or a new surface if it has been physically stuck to other objects before and is still glued together with them or has lost some of its attachment features to something new because of where it has been. Sexual encounters before marriage or outside of what is already a marital relationship affects marriages long after the wedding vows. The brain causes the male and the female to bond physically and psychologically to whoever they are physically intimate with which disrupts marital harmony and the stability of the home or makes it next to impossible to settle down completely with one person. And this is why God wants sex reserved for an actual marriage.

The word fornication comes from the Greek word PORNEA which means sex outside of marriage and the definition includes pre-marital sex, sex by a marriage person with anyone they are not married to, homosexuality and lesbianism, bestiality, sodomy and all other forms of sexual contact.

Jesus said, "Whoever shall put away his wife, except it be for fornication, and shall marry commits adultery." When Jesus said except for fornication, He was talking about sex outside of marriage as being the only cause for divorce. Fornication is all forms of sex outside of a marriage between a man and a woman, which includes adultery, pre-marital sex, and all sexual activity outside of marriage. The Bible says in Genesis 2:24, "Therefore, shall a man leave his father and mother and cleave unto his wife: and they shall be one flesh." And in First Corinthians 7:9 the Bibles says, "But if they cannot contain let them marry: for it is better to marry than to burn." And in First Corinthians 6:18: "Flee fornication for every sin that a man does is without the body; but he that commits fornication sins against his own body." Fornication affects the body and health. The Bible says in First Corinthians 6:13, "Meats for the belly and the belly for meats: but God shall destroy both it and them. Now the body is not for fornication, but for the Lord and the Lord for the body." The Word of God also exhorts us in First Corinthians 7:2, "Nevertheless, to avoid fornication, let every man have his own wife, and let every woman have her own husband." And do not let fornication, uncleanness, or covetousness once be named among you, as you become saints (Eph. 5:3). Jesus said, "For out of the heart proceeds evil thoughts, murders, adulteries, fornication, thefts, false witness, blasphemies: these are things which define a man" (Matt. 15:19).

Finally, in First Corinthians 6:19 the Bible warns that fornicators shall not inherit the kingdom of God. Let no man deceive you with vain words: for because of these things comes the wrath of God upon the children of disobedience (Eph. 5:6).

Repent of all fornication. The Bible says, "Can a man take fire in his bosom and his clothes not be burned? Can one go upon hot coals, and his feet not be burned?" (Prov. 6:27-28) "Who can find a virtuous woman? For her price is far above rubies. The heart of her husband doth safely trust in her, so that he shall have no need of spoil. She will do him good and not evil all the days of her life" (Prov. 31:12).

Jesus says Revelation 2:21-23, "And I gave her space to repent of her fornication; and she repented not. Behold, I will cast her (Jezebel) into a bed, and them that commit adultery with her into great tribulation, except they repent of their deeds. And I will kill her children with death; and the churches shall know that I am he who searches the reins and hearts: and I will give unto every one of you according to your works."

Adulterers Must Repent of Adultery or Are in Danger of Hell Fire

The Bible tells us that marriage is honorable in all and the bed undefiled, but whoremongers and adulterers God will judge (Hebrews 13:4). If you play, you will pay. And in Proverbs 6:32 the Bible says "But whoso commits adultery with a woman lacks understanding: he that doeth it destroys his own soul." Solomon the preacher said in Ecclesiastes 7:26, "I find more bitter than death the woman, whose heart is snares and nets, and her hands as bands: whoso pleases God shall escape her; but the sinner shall be taken by her." He's talking about the kind of woman who hunts for her prey like a black widow spider. Jesus said in Matthew 5:28, "Whosoever looks at a woman to lust after her has committed adultery already in his heart." He also says in Matthew 19:9, "I say unto you, Whosoever shall put away his wife, except it be for fornication, and shall marry commits adultery: and whosoever marries her which is put away doth commit adultery." Again, Solomon said in Proverbs 6:25-26, "Lust not after her beauty in thine heart; neither let her take thee with her eyelids. For by means of a whorish woman a man is brought to a piece of bread: and the adulteress will hunt for the precious life." Adulterers shall not inherit the kingdom of God according to First Corinthians 6:9! Repent of all of the adultery, which has been in your life.

You've probably heard of the biblical story about King David's adultery with Uriah's wife. David saw her bathing and sent for her and later set her husband up to be murdered once she got pregnant to both cover his sin to have her to himself. David greatly repented and we see no record of him committing adultery again. Jesus told the woman that was caught in the act of adultery to go and sin no more. People want God to forgive them, and he will. However people sometimes they won't stop committing adultery or acknowledge that they were wrong. God will bring all adulterers into judgment, if they do not repent of adultery. Committing adultery, then repenting that you've done so, does not give an adulterer a "license" to then go out and do it again, thinking one can always get the matter right later. The Bible says that God is not mocked and that if we sow to the flesh we shall reap corruption. He sees and knows everyone's heart. God says, "Go and sin no more." But if you do sin to the flesh, you shall reap corruption for your flesh (Gal. 6:8). Repent. Time is running out. God is calling every man and woman to repent of adultery. Jesus wants everyone to repent of every thought of adultery and every fantasy, which includes emotional affairs with other men and women that does not involve physical contact. Repent and turn from adultery and escape the wrath of God in hell. Believe that he was nailed to the cross in your place and leave this one alone once and for all. Don't look back as Lot's wife who was hit by the fire and turned to a pillar of salt! The Bible says in Proverbs 30:20, "This is the way of an adulterous woman; she eats, wipes her mouth, and says I have done no wrong." Many adulterers and adulteresses are in denial. He that covers his sin shall not prosper but he that confesses and forsakes it shall obtain mercy (Prov. 28:13).

The Psychological and Physical Motives of Adultery in Men and Women

Research indicates that it is more of an appetite thing for men, the partners that they have in affairs are more disposable to them. Men do not start affairs because they are looking for emotional fulfillment or for attention nor for love but for physical and sexual gratification the vast majority of the time. Men sometimes cheat to get attention, emotional fulfillment, love and romance but it has never been the norm. For men, the act of loving who they want to have an affair with is part of the game and they are aware that women can confuse sex with love or offer the one for the other.

Why do woman cheat? Adultery is normally more like a drug for women and it makes them feel loved and desirable. If a woman has self-esteem issues she is more vulnerable to an affair than other women. Most woman want compliments and attention and reassurance with some flattery and sometimes if she doesn't get it she goes hunting for it.

Sometimes women feel wounded and betrayed by men and wants to get revenge and hurt her husband and she does it because she feels hurt. She also may crave touching, kissing and hugs at home and may begin to look for it elsewhere if she can't find it at home.

Ladies tend to feel that they want to be closer with their husbands and may feel hurt and avoid contact with them. They may also want more affection or attention shown to them by their spouse. They seek attention for emotional fulfillment in the workplace, college, or elsewhere. They will typically be emotionally involved first with whomever they have an affair with and the men may present themselves as friends that they feel confident to confide in and discuss anything with. Once they get involved with affairs ladies may consider divorce or try to end them. They may confuse love with sex or end one affair and start another. They may sometimes promise to themselves they will quit and do the same thing again if they feel their emotional needs are not met at home. They may get angry at their husbands and blame him and think that whoever they are in affairs with are soul-mates and want to other man to divorce their spouses. They are sometimes confused and don't know if they really want to stay with their husbands or not and the husbands will often not be able to detect that an affair is occurring. If they decide to stay with their husbands due to the circumstances they may continue to hide their affairs and stay in them after deciding they may hurt too many people if the truth comes out. They may feel torn between the two (husband and lover) and more often than not married woman have affairs with married men. They may think the other man is more compatible with them than their husbands because they cannot really see the other man up close due to his responsibilities to his own family. They do not confess their adultery due to shame, fear he will get mad at them, insecurity, and often due to the fact that they have not decided whether they want to end the affair and be with the other man or remain in their own marriage especially if they have children. Sometimes both the married woman and the other man who is also married decide to continue the adulterous relationship but keep their families together after deciding too much is at stake as far as careers, reputation, finances, and family ties for the truth to come to the light. Many men are aware than women are vulnerable emotionally and have affection deficit disorder (constant need for revalidation by a male due to self-esteem issues) and they give attention and withdraw attention deliberately to play games with the mind of ladies and to try to break them down emotionally until they have them where they want them. They get caught in the Devil's Trap.

Women in adultery will speak about their husbands in a negative manner to people in their families or friends that they are close to on a routine basis. Because adultery is different for a woman the ladies are more likely to want a divorce if they are in an affair than the men. Men for the most part are able to differentiate love with sex but for a lot of woman one is an indicator of the other and they both go hand in hand.

The Strange Woman

She is the married cougar. As you read the seventh chapter of Proverbs you find that a young man passed through the street near the corner of the house of a strange woman. It was twilight in the black and dark night. The woman had on the clothing of a harlot and the Bibles says she was subtle (deceitful) of heart. The Bible never says she was a harlot but that she had on the outfit of a harlot. She was deceitful and had her own agenda. She was also loud and stubborn which describes her personality. The Bible also said that she would not remain at her own house. She would wander from corner to corner and wait to meet a man. She was an attention seeker and he was a thrill seeker. She caught the man and kissed him and told him that her bed was decked with coverings and the linen of Egypt and perfume. She is trying to seduce him through his senses (sight, hearing, smell). She then set's him a trap and allures him to come to her house until the morning. She says the Goodman (Old English word for husband) is gone on a long journey. The Bible says, "with her fair speech she caused him to yield, with the flattery of her lips she forced him." She manipulated his mind and he slept with her and he was seduced due to her psychological force. All men must listen carefully to how this chapter in the Bible ends when you think of this type of a woman. You are not the only man she has played this game with. The Bible says in Proverbs 7:26-27, "For she has cast down many wounded; yea, many strong men have been slain (murdered) by her. Her house is the way to hell, going down to the chambers of death." These types of women are good about getting you to think you are the only one and that you are their king. Ladies must repent of playing the role of a seductress especially when they are married. Men must repent of seeking her out and of yielding to her flattery, beauty, and her game of seduction and deceit. The Bible says in the book of Proverbs in chapter 5 and verse 5 "Her feet go down to death; her steps take hold on hell." Repent. Believe the gospel. Run from her and don't go near her house or corner. It's not a treat but a trick and a trap. The Devil wants to have your soul. Eve was deceived by the Devil. Adam was not deceived and voluntarily sinned because he got seduced by a woman.

Selfish People

God destroyed the cities of Sodom and Gomorrah for failing to aid the needy. The Bible says in Ezekiel 16:49, "Behold, this was the iniquity of thy sister Sodom, pride, fullness of bread, and abundance of idleness was in her and in her daughters, neither did she strengthen the hand of the poor and needy. And they were haughty and committed abomination before me; therefore I took them away as I saw good."

Once you read the twenty fifth chapter of the book of Matthew you find that Jesus described the goat in his left hand as those who done nothing for the sick, prisoners, strangers, the hungry, the thirsty, and the least of them. God does not forget the sins of omission and how people were able to really lift others up but refused to help them when it was in the power of their hand to do so. He tells them in the end to depart from him into everlasting fire prepared for the devil and his angels.

False Converts Planted in the Church by the Devil

In Matthew 13:24-42 Jesus said that the tares among the wheat which Satan planted in local churches may resemble Christians but shall be separated from the true converts and gathered together at the end of the world and thrown into a furnace of fire by the angels. They are described as those that offend and do iniquity in verse 41 of chapter 13. Undoubtedly, some of them could be rapists, murderers, thieves, liars, deceivers, fornicators, adulterers, extortionists, haters, sorcerers, whoremongers, hypocrites, and others who did not truly repent of their sins from their hearts or sincerely believe the gospel.

False Teachers

In Second Peter 2:1-21, the Bible tells us that false teachers in the church shall have damnation. It describes that the false preachers as Balaam, have forsaken the right way and have gone astray. Their judgment has been lingering for a long time and their damnation is not asleep but is waiting (2 Peter 2:3). This chapter also warns us that God did not spare the angels that sinned, but cast them down to hell, and He spared not the world during the days of Noah, but destroyed them with a flood, except Noah and his family, and turned Sodom and Gomorrah into ashes as an example for the ungodly to come. False teachers are leading souls to the lake of fire. What then shall be the destiny of the false pastors and teachers? Jesus warned that if the blind lead the blind that they both would fall into the ditch together. Run out of those churches if they won't share the full gospel truth about sin, hell, repentance, faith, the final judgment, and the one way of salvation from sin through Jesus Christ. Run. Run as if your life and your soul were in jeopardy.

The Hypocrite

In Matthew 7:21-23 Jesus said, "Not every one that says Lord, Lord, shall enter into the Kingdom of Heaven; but he that doeth the will of My Father which is in heaven. Many will say to me in that day, Lord, Lord, have we not prophesied in Thy Name? and in Thy Name cast out devils? And in Thy name done many wonderful works? And then I will profess unto them, I never knew you: depart from me, ye that work iniquity." Even so ye outwardly appear righteous unto men, but within ye are full of hypocrisy and iniquity (Matt. 23:28).

Many people come to church for many reasons. Some may be looking for a husband or wife. Some look at it as a social club. Others come because they enjoy dressing up or being noticed or because it is a family tradition or a habit. People may come to be entertained or they may come to hear a good word of encouragement or a motivational speech. Some may want to use others for profit and material gain. Jesus said the people honored him with their lips but their hearts were far from him and that the prophet Isaiah had spoken accurately of them.

Many Preachers will go to Hell

The Bible says, "For such are false apostles and deceitful workers, transforming themselves into the apostles of Christ. And marvel not, for Satan himself is transformed into an angel of light. Therefore, it is no great thing if his ministers, also be transformed as the ministers of righteousness: whose end shall be according to their works" (I Corinthians 11:13-15). The false preacher, Apostle, Pastor or minister will not enter into heaven. Satan's ministers will not tell the truth or even proclaim that repentance or even bother to mention that hell and the wrath of God is coming. Jesus said, "Many false prophets shall arise and deceive many" (Matt. 24:11). He also said, "Fear not them which can kill the body but are not able to destroy the soul: but rather fear him which is able to destroy body and soul in hell" (Matt. 10:28).

Sadly, many preachers will be in hell. Why? Because they were deceivers, manipulators and con artists and they were not called or sent by God. They brought into the church heresies (false doctrine) and misled the people. Many entered into the pulpits simply for profit and gain and were the wolf in sheep's clothing that Jesus warned us would come (Matt. 7:15). We often hear the false preachers and don't even realize that they are not the true ministers of God. A wolf with the outfit of the sheep on can look just like one of the sheep. They may fool many Christians but they won't fool God. The agenda of the wolf in sheep's clothing is to con the souls out of money in order to get rich. The wolf comes to fleece the sheep. The prophet Ezekiel said, "When I say unto the wicked, you shall surely die; and thou give him not warning, nor speak to warn the wicked to turn from his wicked way, to save his life, the same wicked man shall die in his iniquity; but his blood will I require at thy hand" (Ezek. 3:18). God shall require each preacher to answer to him regarding their ministries. The prophet said the blood will be on our hand if we don't warn the wicked to turn from his wicked way. Many think their Pastors or preachers are sincere because they mention the Bible and Jesus but can forget that Satan himself quoted scripture to Jesus.

The preachers that have damnation waiting are described in Second Peter 2:1-22. According to Second Peter 2:20-22, the Bible says, "For if they after they have escaped the pollutions of the world through the knowledge of the Lord Jesus Christ, they are again entangled therein, and overcame, the latter end is worse with them than the beginning. For it had been better for them not to have known the way of righteousness than, after they have known it, to turn from the holy commandment delivered unto them. But it happened according to the true proverb, the dog is turned to his own vomit again; and the sow that was washed to her wallowing in the mire." The wrath of God in Hell is greater for the one who knew the commandments of God and willfully violated them while knowing the truth. We sometimes hear stories of preachers backsliding into the world and doing many things to include lying, adultery, drugs, and stealing. They cannot enter into heaven unless they repent again. They may not find repentance. The Bible says in Second Peter 2:15-16, "Which have forsaken the right way, and are gone astray, following the way of Balaam the prophet, son of Bosor, who loved the wages of unrighteousness; but was rebuked for his iniquity; the dumb ass speaking with man's voice forbade the madness of the prophet." Balaam was a self-willed prophet who ran ahead of God and went to Moab in order to get paid money. The self-will and God's will are two different things. The Bible says, "And through covetousness shall they make merchandise of you: whose judgment for a long time lingereth not, and their damnation slumbers not" (2 Peter 2:3). Balaam was the prophet for hire who went to Moab solely to get paid and the get the monetary compensation that came along with it. "But there were false prophets (ministers) also among the people, even there shall be false teachers among you, who shall bring in damnable heresies, (false teaching) even denying the Lord that bought them, and brings upon themselves swift destruction. Having eyes full of adultery, and that cannot cease from sin (stop); beguiling unstable souls; a heart they have exercised with covetous practices; cursed children" (2 Peter 2:14). These versus indicate that false teachers shall use the people as merchandise to make money. In order to fool the multitudes they have to teach false doctrines that sound like the true Bible message. Nevertheless, this false doctrine is packaged with lies and deception to trick the people out of their money. The Bible does not teach men and women to covet money, houses, wealth, and the material things of the world. The people who do these things are called idolaters and no idolater hath any inheritance in the Kingdom of God (I Corinthains 6:9). The Bible does not teach men and women to give money with the sole intent of receiving from God or from others.

Jesus said that we cannot serve both God and money (Matthew 6:24). Jesus also taught to beware of covetousness and that a man's life did not consist in the abundance of things he owned (Luke 12:15). He told the Rich Young Ruler to give his money to the poor to have treasure in heaven. We are told by Jesus to pray that his will is done on the earth as it is in heaven but not to pray a selfish prayer. Therefore, it is inconsistent with God's word that we ask for something in prayer based on our own selfish motives or desires which is the very reason why prayers go unanswered by God (James 4:3). The Word of God has warned, "Perverse disputings of men of corrupt minds, and destitute of the truth, supposing that gain is godliness: from such withdraw thyself. But godliness with contentment is great gain (I Timothy 6:5-6). Jesus told us to seek first the kingdom of God and his righteousness and that all of those other things that the Gentiles sought after would be added to us after we sought him and his righteousness first (Matthew 6:33). I am not opposed to giving but if we give to ministries with the hope that God will give to us the things of the temporal world our motivation for giving is wrong. Satan's charge against Job to God was that Job served God for selfish motives (Job 1:1-14). The worship of God must be pure and unadulterated by idolatry and the covetousness to get the things of the world from God. God is not our Santa Claus or a genie in a bottle to grant us each worldly request that we have.

The Apostle Paul declared that after he had preached to others that he put his own body in subjection in order that he himself should not be a castaway (1 Cor. 9:27). Preachers are in danger of the flames of hell if the lusts of their own flesh have caused them to fall into sins in which they can find no repentance for. The Bible says, "While they promise them liberty, they themselves are the servants of corruption; for of whom a man is overcome, of the same is he brought into bondage" (2 Peter 2:19). God is calling every preacher, teacher, apostle, prophet, pastor, minister, and spiritual leader to repent. "Repent and turn from your transgressions so that iniquity shall not be your ruin" (Ezek. 18:30). "The heart is deceitful above all things, and desperately wicked: who can know it?" (Jer. 17:9) "I the Lord search the heart; I try the reins, even to give every man according to his ways, and according to the fruit of his doings." (Jer. 17:10).

Unprofitable Servants and Slothful Servants

The Bible teaches that the unprofitable servant that took his talent that God gave him, hid it by burying it in the sand, will be thrown into outer darkness and there shall be wailing and gnashing of teeth (Matthew 25:30).

Jesus said, "And that servant, which knew his lord's will and prepared not himself, neither did according to his will, shall be beaten with many stripes" (Luke 12:47).

God wants us to use whatever talents or gifts that He's given us for Him and the kingdom of God. God has given us an assignment. He wants us to be faithful to that assignment and to do according to His will. We must ask ourselves the question as to what specifically does Jesus want us to do with the time He has given us. We have our own will but what is the will of God for our life?

The Deceived

Don't fall for the lies of that old flattering serpent. Revelation 20:2-3 informs us that the dragon, the old serpent, Satan that deceived the nations shall be thrown into the bottomless pit. Many that will go to hell do not believe that they are going to hell. Somewhere in life, Satan fooled them into thinking that although they had rejected Jesus, refused to repent or had practiced serving Satan that they could still go to heaven and everything would be just fine. Not everyone that says Lord, Lord, shall enter into the kingdom of the Lord according to Matthew 7:21-23 but only those that do the will of the Father. They were fooled and deceived in their own minds and their very souls. Straight is the gate and narrow is the way and few there be that find it. Wide is the gate and broad is the way to destruction and many go therein. (See Matthew 7:13-14.) Are you on the narrow way or the broad way? Which gate did you go through the wide gate or the straight gate? Don't be fooled. Are you caught in the snare of the Devil? Are you trapped in one of his nets?

The Commandment Breakers

The Bible exhorts, "Know ye not that the unrighteous shall not inherit the Kingdom of God? Be not deceived: neither fornicators (those who continue to practice having premarital sexual relations), nor idolaters (those that worship money or have earthly things as their priority), nor adulterers (those women or men that have sexual contact with people outside of their marriage and are often slipping off into little motels together), nor the effeminate (these are the men who act like they are women, or those that may dress up like them, having the qualities generally attributed to women, as weakness, timidity, delicacy, etc.; unmanly...), nor abusers of themselves with mankind (homosexuals), nor thieves (it doesn't matter if you stole only a penny. If you stole just a penny you are a thief because you violated God's law), nor covetous (the people who want to have things that belong to someone else, or that envy others); nor drunkards (the people who get drunk all the time), nor revilers (those troublemakers that cause trouble whenever they open up their mouth, they create confusion and chaos); nor extortioners (the people that obtain money or property illegally including drug dealers, prostitutes, pimps, con artists and those that are running scams) shall not inherit the Kingdom of God" (I Corinthians 6:9). The word effeminate refers to homosexuals and is translated as homosexuals in other translations of your Bible. Almost every place you can find a thief trying to sell you something, he's stolen it from somewhere. Confess with your mouth that these are sins to Jesus. Repent of these sins in your heart and believe the good news of the gospel of Jesus Christ. It is the only way the escape the wrath of God in the lake that burns with fire and brimstone. Time is running out and it is appointed unto us once to die and after that the judgment!

Haters

Many people reveal that they are not Christians by the hatred with their hearts. The Word of God says, "Whosoever hates his brother is a murderer; and no murderer has eternal life abiding in him" (1 John 3:15). "If a man says I love God and hate his brother he is a liar: for he that loves not his brother whom he has seen, how can he love God whom he has not seen?" (1 John 4:20) People in churches can hate one another just as much as people on the street that don't even know God. Many true men and woman of God are hated, lied on, scandalized, and defamed. Racism is hatred. Hatred kills, divides, and destroys. People can hate others because of envy, jealousy, covetousness, and greed. Repent of all hatred at once. The Bible says, "The hypocrite with lying lips hides hatred.

The Unmerciful That Won't Forgive Others

Jesus said, "If ye forgive men not their trespasses neither will your Father forgive your trespasses" (Matt. 6:15). You may have a little black book with a list of things that someone has done wrong against you and you may be holding those things against them instead of letting them go, and if that is the case, God will hold His record book that has your sins recorded in it against you. You are not God. You cannot hold a record book of things against anyone and then expect God to forget his record book on you. If you don't forgive, you cannot be forgiven by God and cannot go to heaven. Repent of all bitterness and unforgiveness in your hearts. Let it go to escape the wrath of God to come. Forgiving others does not mean you approve of what they've done nor does it mean that you can be reconciled with them. However, we must repent of all of those times that we held a grudge against someone in our hearts even if they did not know about it. Let it go. Yes you were offended but we have offended many people ourselves and we have offended God. God expects us to forgive those that offended us if we expect Him to forgive us for offending Him!

Jesus Died for Our Sins and That is the Good News

The good news is that nobody has to go to Hell. Jesus lived a perfect life for us and gave us credit for being righteous based on the life he lived. Jesus also suffered and died for us to pay for the penalty of our sins in order for us to have eternal life. We are forgiven once we repent and believe the gospel.

Let us understand together how the fact that Jesus died for us enables us to escape eternal damnation in hell. The key is to believe the good news and to turn to Jesus with a heart of repentance. How does Jesus save us? He saves us by dismissing the charges that were proven against us and by nailing the entire record of our sins to the cross. The prophet Isaiah said, "Come now, and let us reason together, saith the Lord: though your sins be as scarlet, they shall be as white as snow; though they be red like crimson, they shall be as wool" (Isa. 1:18).

The death of Jesus and His blood cleanses you from all sin and guilt and sets you free from God's penalty for sin, which is eternal damnation in the lake of fire. FAITH in his finished work on the cross washes our sins away and makes them white as snow in God's sight once we repent and believe and surrender our life to him. The Bible says, "For this is my blood of the New Testament, which is shed for many for the remission of sins" (Matthew 26:28 KJV) or "For this is my blood, sealing the New Covenant. It is poured out to forgive the sins of the multitudes" (TLB). The ordinances which proves that you are guilty of sin were in fact nailed to the cross and abolished (Colossians 2:14).

Therefore, the sacrifice of Jesus for us on the cross with his blood that was shed causes us to be delivered from the curse of the law, which is eternal death and *separation* from God. It makes a way for us to get to heaven although we have broken his law and the commandments. The blood of Jesus also causes us to be able to inherit the promises of God by faith.

The Bible says, "But Christ has bought us out from under the doom of that impossible system by taking care of the curse for our wrongdoing upon Himself. For it is written in the Scripture, "Anyone who was hanged on a tree is cursed." (Just as Jesus was HUNG upon a WOODEN CROSS) (TLB) (Galations 3:13).The King James versions says it like this "Christ hath redeemed us from the curse of the law, (penalties from breaking God's commandments) being made a curse for us: for it is written, Cursed is every one that hangs on a tree" (Galations 3:13). Jesus had to come to earth to set us free from the laws which doomed us to eternity in hell. The Bible teaches, "But when the right time came, the time God decided on, he sent his Son, born of a woman, born as a Jew, to buy freedom for us who were slaves to the law (requirements to follow Old Testament rules in order to be saved and escape penalties) so that he could adopt us as his very own sons" (Galations 4:4-5 TLB). Again, the scriptures teach, "But when the fullness of time was come, God sent forth his Son, made of a woman, made under the law, to redeem them that were under the law, that we might receive the adoption of sons" (Galations 4:4-5 KJV).

Jesus does not condemn us because he is the one who died for us. He makes it very unlikely that we will be sentenced to hell once we repent and believe. The death of Jesus Christ and his shed blood delivers us from condemnation once we repent and believe. People do not have the right to hold anything against us because God has forgiven us. All sins and penalties are erased and blotted out. The death was for any of our future sins also which he promised to forgive and cleanse us from if we confessed them to him and asked (I John 1:9). We also cannot condemn others or condemn ourselves if we believe that Jesus truly has paid the price for us and them. Jesus said, "He that believes on him is not condemned: but he that believes not is condemned already, because he has not believed in the name of the only begotten Son of God" (John 3:18).

The Bible says, "Who then will condemn us? Will Christ? No! For he is the one who died for us and came back to life again for us and is sitting at the place of highest honor next to God, pleading for us there in heaven" (Romans 8:34 TLB). The King James versions puts it like this, "Who is he that condemneth? It is Christ that died, yea rather, that is risen again, who is even at the right hand of God, who also maketh intercession for us" (KJV).

The love of Jesus for us was shown by his sacrificial death and his blood, which was shed for us, makes us worthy to be accepted by God, and reconciled to Him with peace once we repent of our sins, confess, and believe the Gospel.

It was through what his Son did that God cleared the path for everything to come to him. All things in heaven and earth, for Christ's death on the cross have made peace with God for all by his blood (Colossians 1:20). The peace comes when one repents and believe the good news. The Word of God declares, "And, having made peace through the blood of his cross, by him to reconcile all things unto himself; by him, I say, whether they be things in earth, or things in heaven" (KJV).Jesus became sin for us and was nailed to the cross in our place; the ungodly who doesn't have the strength to do what is right in God's eyes can now be saved. The Bible teaches, "For he hath made him to be sin for us, who knew no sin; that we might be made the righteousness of God in him" (II Corinthians 5:21).

The Bible teaches, "When we were utterly helpless with no way of escape, Christ came at just the right time and died for us sinners who had no use for him" (Romans 5:6 TLB). For when we were yet without strength, in due time Christ died for the ungodly (KJV Romans 5:6).

As we live our life now and know that we are depending on the Grace of God to save us we look forward to heaven and a peaceful entrance to our heavenly home. The death of Jesus Christ and his blood delivers us from the power of death and from having to literally taste death. We therefore, should not fear death and can have joy regarding our loved ones who have departed and hope beyond the grave The Bible says, "And now he has made all of this plain to us by the coming of our Savior Jesus Christ, who broke the power of death and showed us the way of everlasting life through trusting him" (II Timothy 1:10 TLB). We may not understand everything but we trust Jesus to save us and to finish what he started with us. The scripture declare, "But is now made manifest by the appearing of our Savior Jesus Christ, who hath abolished death, and hath brought life and immortality to light through the gospel" (KJV).Jesus died for the entire world and this should inspire us to share this with all. The Bible says,

"But we do see Jesus, who for a while was a little lower than the angels, crowned with glory and honor because he suffered death for us. Yes, because of God's great kindness, Jesus tasted death for everyone in the entire world" (Hebrews 2:9 TLB).The life of Jesus and him laying down his life for us pays our debt of punishment which we owe to God. Christ and his death delivers us from the judgment and wrath of God to come, including hell's wrath and the Lake of Fire and brimstone, if we repent, confess, and believe the Gospel of Jesus Christ. The fruit in our lives of righteous works and holy living is a work performed through us by the Holy Spirit. We become new creatures but only because Jesus walks through us to cleanse us from our own sins.People must be cautious with charging God's child and holding something against them especially if God has forgiven them. The scriptures teach, "Who shall lay any thing to the charge of God's elect? It is God that justifieth" (I Thessalonians 1:10 TLB).I want you to notice the transition that took place with the new Christian. The Bible says, "For they themselves, shew of us what manner of entering in we had unto you, and how you turned to God from idols to serve the living and true God; And to wait for his son from heaven, whom he raised from the dead, even Jesus, which delivered us from the wrath to come" (I Thessalonians 1:9-10 KJV). The Living Bible says, "For God has not chosen to pour out his anger upon us, but to save us through our Lord Jesus Christ; he died for us so that we can live with him forever, whether we are dead or alive at the time of his return" (TLB).The charges which were proven against you have been dismissed and thrown out of the God's courtroom. The death of Jesus Christ abolishes and dismisses the charges and accusations against us by people and by Satan, our accuser, and puts us in a just standing before God.

The worst of sinners can be saved because of the sacrificial death of Jesus in their place. He made the way for unjust men to be saved and brought to heaven with God. He makes it possible for all unlikely persons to get to heaven. The Bible says "Christ also, suffered. He died once for the sins of all us guilty sinners, although he himself was innocent of any sin at any time, that he might bring us safely home to God" (I Peter 3:18 TLB).

The wrath of God and the fires of hell are avoidable because of the death of Jesus Christ. The death of Jesus is what justifies you in the sight of God and by His blood you are considered righteous and saved from the wrath of God in hell. We must simply repent and believe. The Bible says, "And since by his blood he did all this for us as sinners, how much more will he do for us now that he has declared us not guilty? Now he will save us from all of God's wrath to come" (Romans 5:9 TLB). The King James Version says it like this, "Much more then, being now justified by his blood, we shall be saved from wrath through him" (KJV).

As we think about Hell and who is going it is great news that a sinner won't go if he repents and believes the gospel. He must be forgiven. The Bible says, "Who bought our freedom with his blood and forgave us all our sins" (Colossians 1:14 TLB). The Colossian writer also testified, "Blotting out the charges proved against you, the list of commandments which you had not obeyed. He took this list of sins and destroyed it by nailing it to the cross. In this way God took away Satan's power to accuse you of sin, and God openly displayed to the whole world Christ's triumph at the cross where your sins were taken away" (Colossians 2:14-15 TLB). The King James Version says it like this, "Blotting out the handwriting of ordinances that was against us, which was contrary to us, and took it out of the way, nailing it to the cross. And having spoiled principalities and powers, he made a shew of them openly, triumphing over them in it" (Colossians 2:14-15).

As we surrender our lives to Jesus we have no need to constantly fear the idea of dying. We have eternal life and will life forever with Jesus once we repent and believe. The death of Jesus once understood, delivers us all from the bondage of the fear of death because of our understanding that we have eternal life and will live forever with Him. The best of everything is yet to come. He said, "I go to prepare a place for you and if I go to prepare a place for you I will come again and receive you to myself. In my father's house are many mansions" (John 14:1-3). The Bible says, Hebrews 2:14-15: "Since we, God's children are human beings, made of flesh and blood, he became flesh and blood too by being born in human form; for only as a human being could, he died and in dying broke the power of the devil who had the power of death. Only in that way could he deliver those who through the fear of death have been living all their lives as slaves to constant dread" (Hebrews 2:14-15 TLB).

We are healed from health problems. We are health from the infirmities of our mind. We are healed from guilt, depression, shame, fear, worry, and hopelessness. The death of Jesus Christ and His blood was God's substitute for your punishment, which was deserved. The work of Jesus Christ sets us free from bondage to our spiritual enemies (devils), which torment the mind. It causes you to be healed *if you believe*. The Bible declares, "But he was wounded and bruised for our sins. He was beaten that we might have peace; he was lashed, and we are healed" (Isaiah 53:5 TLB). The King James Version says it like this, "But he was wounded for our transgressions, he was bruised for our iniquities: the chastisement of our peace was upon him; and with his stripes we are healed" (KJV).

We, every one of us, strayed away like sheep. We, who left God's path to follow our own, Yet God, have laid on him the guilt and sins of every one of us" (Isaiah 53:6 TLB). The Bible says, "All we like sheep have gone astray; we have turned every one to his own way; and the Lord hath laid on him the iniquity of us all" (KJV).

The Good News is that once we confess our sins to God, re-pent with godly sorrow by changing our mind and turning to Jesus, believe the good news of the death, burial, and resurrec-tion of Jesus for us, and surrender our life to Him as a born again believer we are then set free from guilt, condemnation, the curse of the law, disease, the penalty of sins, spiritual death, hell's re-ality, and the wrath of God to come. We are free from the things which will be poured out upon His enemies in hell and the Lake of Fire. Jesus paid the price for our sins and enables us to receive all of God's blessings and the good things, which He has in store for us, both in this life and in the life to come. Our soul is healed from the bondage of the fear of death, guilt, shame, depression, confusion, and we are liberated from all of our spiritual enemies. They are demons. We inherit his promises by faith which gives us hope to receive all things in this life that are good from God which includes being prosperous and in good health. We will also have our share of trouble, tribulation, trials, rain, and perse-cution but we know his plan ensures that we should be brought safely home with Him. Be confident that the Lord that has begun a good work in you shall continue to perform that work until the day of Jesus Christ (Philippians 1:6).

Bibliography

Baldwin, W.J (1991) Spirit Releasement Therapy: A Technique Manual (2nd Ed.) Falls Church, VA: The Human Potential Foundation Press.

Bush, N.E., The near death experience in children. Shades of the prison-house reopening. The Journal of Near-Death Studies (1983) 3:177.93.

Bush, N.E., (2002) Afterward: making meaning after a frightening near-death experience. Journal of near- death experience. Journal of Near Death Studies, 21(2), 99-133.

Bush, N.E. (2006) Distressing Western N.D.E's Research Summary. Paper presented at the IANDS Conference, M.D. Anderson Hospital, Houston (DVD available)

"Dead man Raised from the Dead by famed Doctor's prayer." (February 29, 2008) Video Clip, Accessed January 2012. Youtube.www.youtube.com. http://www.youtube.com/watch?v=RRoAcFzytCA. Uploaded by FreeCDTracts.

Fiorce, E. (1987) The Unquiet Dead: A Psychologist treats Spirit Possession. New York. Ballantine Books.

Greyson and Bush, N.E. (1992) Distressing Near Death Experiences, Psychiatry, 55, 95-109.

Greyson B., and Stevenson, I. The phenomenology of near-death experiences. American Journal of Psychiatry (1980) 137:1193-1196.

Grey, M. Return from Death: An Exploration of Near-Death Experience. Arkana (1985).

Grosso, M. Toward an explanation of near-death phenomena. Journal of the American Society of Psychical Research (1981) 75:37-60.

Healing for the Soul: An Enigma Unraveled by Pastor Eric A. Folds copyright 2012.

Hickman, I. (1994) Remote Depossession. Kirksville, MO . Hickman Systems.

"Man dies and comes back to life." (n.d.) Video clip, Accessed January 2012. Youtube.www.youtube.com. http://www.youtube.com/watch?v=9MIDKD7yw

Man dies and comes back to life, what he saw. Uploaded by TheLeegoodall on Nov 5, 2009. http//www.youtube.com/watch/v=xRSjzYOsO5m. I did not review this site in preparation of sermon notes but I propose that this site is reviewed by the reader for another example of proof of the afterlife and of the reality of heaven and hell.

"Miracle Reinhard Bonnke Tells of Nigerian Man Raised from the Dead." (n.d.), Video Clip,AccessedJanuary2012.Youtube. www.youtube.com. http://www.cbn.com/700club/features/bonnke-raisedpastor.aspx.

"New Science Now Proves Jesus Christ." (February, 13, 2010) Video Clip, Accessed June2010.Youtube. www.youtube.com.http://www.youtube.com/watch?v_AJPL8PxcwIY&feature=related. Uploaded by uvideosu.

"New Science Now Proves Jesus Christ." (February, 13, 2010) Video Clip, Accessed June2010.Youtube.www.youtube.com/watch?v_AJPL8PxcwIY&Feature=related. Uploaded by uvideosu.

"Quantum Awakening-Have Science found God?" (May 19,2009) Video clip, Accessed November2012.Youtube.www. youtube.com/watch/?v=n426pazcFXE.Uploadedby ppSimmons. I strongly recommend this site for your viewing.

"Raised from the Dead." (November 6, 2006) Video Clip, Accessed January 2012. Youtube.www.youtube.com.http://www. youtube.com/watch?v=tc6EGHhyUeY&Feature=related.

"Raising the Dead by Dr. Crandall on CBN 915 10." (September 10, 2010) Video Clip, Accessed January 2012. Youtube.www. youtube.com/watch?v=EL@i64j2FZE.

Bonnke, Reinhard (October 7, 2008) Raised from the Dead Video Clip, Accessed Dec2011.youtube.www.youtube.com.http//www. youtube.com/watch?v=13Y7wT20mmw24&feature=related. Uploaded by Nowlistening.

Science Discovers God: The Mystery of Quantum Physics and Light, Folds, Eric (2013). Xulon Press. Scientists "Jesus Rose from the Dead" Astounding Proof! (n.d.) Video Clip, AssessedJune2011andJanuary2012.Youtube.www.youtube.com/ watch?v=voTiCTqv4Q&feature=related.

"Shroud of Jesus Proof of Resurrection." (September 16, 2008) Video Clip, Assessed June2010.Youtube.www.youtube.com/ watch?v=AkDFKnxtSOk.Uploaded byVideoArchives.

"Turin Scientifically proves the resurrection by Dr. Richard Kent" (n.d.) Video Clip, AssessedNovember2011.Youtube.www. youtube.com/watch?v=ClIZA9AOZGK. Uploaded by FreeChrist.

Zaleski, C. Otherworld Journeys. Accounts of Near-Death Experience in Medieval and Modern Times. Oxford University Press. 1987.

CPSIA information can be obtained
at www.ICGtesting.com
Printed in the USA
LVHW111411110621
690000LV00012B/79

9 781629 991184